MONEY

HOW TO GET IT
HOW TO KEEP IT

IDA GREENE, Ph.D.

ISBN 1-881165-18-3

ATTENTION COLLEGES AND UNIVERSITIES, CORPORATIONS, AND PROFESSIONAL ORGANIZATIONS:
Quantity discounts are available on bulk purchases of this book for educational training purposes, fund raising, or gift giving. contact:
P. S. I. Publishers,
2910 Baily Ave.
San Diego, CA 92105
(619) 262-9951

Dr. Ida Greene, RN, Marriage, Family, Child Counselor has established a non-profit organization called, Our Place Center of Self-Esteem, which assists at-risk children, and families coping with issues of violence and abuse. A portion of the sale from each book is donated to at-risk youths of Our Place Center of Self-Esteem. Dr. Greene speaks, and conducts seminars, on personal/professional growth topics.

Other publications by Dr. Greene are:

Books

Light the Fire Within You

Soft Power Negotiation Skills™

How to Be A Success In Business

How To Improve Self-Esteem In The African American Child.

Audio Cassettes:

Money, How to Get, How To Keep It

Light The Fire Within You.

Video Cassette:

Self-Esteem, The Essence Of You.

For information please contact Dr. Greene at:

P. S. I. Publishers
2910 Baily Avenue
San Diego, CA 92105
(619) 262-9951

Acknowledgements

I Wish To Thank The Following:

My mother who encouraged me to get an education, and my father who showed me how to be an entrepreneur, both are deceased.

In Pensacola, Florida where I grew up, I thank:My fifth and sixth grade teachers, Mrs. Bascom, my eighth grade teacher, Mrs. Ragland, tenth, eleventh and twelfth grade teacher; Mrs. E. B. Debose, all who saw my potential before I was aware of it. My college advisor, Dr. I. N. McCollom, for helping me to stretch beyond my limitations to reach for higher goals, and to God for implanting within me a spirit of power, courage and a sound mind.

Ida Greene

The Road to Financial Success

I believe there is a natural impulse within all creation to evolve, expand and refine itself, we either stagnate and die or better ourselves and live, more productive and fuller lives. All nature tells us to change and evolve. Notice the leaves on a tree as they move from a flower blossom to a leaf, and the seasons of the year as they go from cool to warm and wet to dry. Nothing ever remains the same including our body. It works continuously to digest, assimilate and maintain a state of normalcy regardless of the kinds of food we eat.

There is a peculiar characteristic about us humans that make us want to better our condition and improve our lifestyle. God has implanted within us, a striving to be more, to strive for completion and wholeness, the foundation on which is self-esteem, self-confidence, and faith in a power greater than ourselves. Many of us seek to make changes in our outer lives yet fail to listen to our inner prompting. Yet there are others, who, only want to eat, sleep, and live a life of quiet desperation, futility, hopelessness, and helplessness. We were born to procreate and create, to improve our life and the lives of others through the accomplishment of our dreams and aspirations in life.

When we become better, those around us become better also. Therefore, it is in the best interest of society, for all of us to want more out of life, to strive to improve our life and the lives of those around us. This is what success is all about. Success is the progressive realization of a worthwhile goal and the attainment of that goal. When we are actively pursuing a goal, it brings joy, hope and excitement into our lives. There is an exhilaration of love, compassion and understanding for others. It all begins with us helping us. However, we must feel worthwhile and deserving of something better in life for it to become a reality in our life. The road to success is beset with obstacles and seeming challenges. This is good, for it gives us an opportunity to employ the principles of faith, hope and confidence.

Maybe you are thinking that financial success is for a chosen few and you are not one of them. If this is your thinking, begin now to erase that idea from your mind. Money, opulence abundance and wealth is a natural state for all of us. There is always three types of success that we are working on in a given time period. They are Personal, Financial Spiritual and Social. There is a large overlap of the financial/money into the other three aspects of our live. Money is tied to survival, so it comes more frequent in our life.

You will need to decide what type of success is right for you at this point in your life. It may be personal success, where you work on your relationships with others or spiritual success, whereby you decide if there is a Supreme Power in the universe and discover your relationship to that power. On the other hand, you may need an improvement in financial success, to better provide for your family's daily needs or give more money to your church or favorite charity. Whatever the reason, financial success awaits you, it is your innate drive to want more, so you can improve the lives of other. Therefore this book will focus on what it will take for you to Get Money and Keep Money.

Ida Greene

Contents

Chapter I

Are You Ready For Financial Success?

What is Financial Success? Financial Success is whatever you want it to be. Financial Success is your ability to dream or imagine something in your mind, and then create that in the physical realm, from the un-manifest to the manifest. Success is any dream, desire, goals you long for and eventually achieve. Your desires may be personal, professional, spiritual or a combination of all you desire. We are by nature, goal seeking, goal striving individuals. If we are not seeking ways to improve ourselves on a personal, professional and spiritual level, decay of the mind sets in, and we begin to die slowly.

It is the nature of the human species to evolve, improve, and perfect its flaws or deficiencies. When this does not happen stagnation occurs in our physiological system, in the form of disease, slow degeneration and cell destruction until all the cells in our body no longer gives off energy or light. We then return to our original form of dust, "ashes to ashes and dust to dust."

The natural progression of the human species is birth→ goal seeker/goal striving→ movement→ energy→ excitement→ enthusiasm→ aliveness→ light→ contentment→ love→ joy→ bliss→ peace with oneself, one's God and all species on planet earthg end of reincarnationg eternal life. The unnatural progression of the human species is birth→ unhealthy living is anger, hostility, chemical/substance/emotional/physical abuse, fear, low self-worth/esteem/confidence, lack, limitation, lack of faith in God/Supreme Being/isolation/aloneness/no spiritual support, confusiong lack of trust in others→ disorganization→ destruction→ apathy→ emotional death→ physiological death→ disintegration→ reincarnation to learn unlearned lessons and end the birth to death cycle of life.

Are You Ready for Financial Success?

Many of us would rather do anything but improve our financial circumstances. There is a perception that to have money involves hard work and a denial of pleasure. What will it require for you to take action to make your dreams becomes a reality?. To have more money, will require that you do several things: Increase your faith factor, have a strong belief in a divine benevolent power to sustain and support you, that you are willing to do all you can humanly do, know when to let go, so God can guide you in the right direction, be open to miracles and know that nothing is impossible for you and God together as a team.

Be willing to learn, grow emotionally, intellectually, spiritually and financially. Any negative deeply embedded mental programming you have about money will surface, so watch your thoughts whenever you touch money. Be willing to change your beliefs about money and money substance. The use of affirmations can help to reprogram your mind. Remember money is a tool that can be used for good to help humanity. Begin to think and silently say to yourself "money is a tool that I can use, to improve the quality of life for myself as well as others. Remember, who and what you are.

<u>What you are is God's gift to you. What you make of yourself is your gift to God</u>. On the basis of this premise answer the following question below. Write whatever comes to your mind, do not write what you think someone wants you to say or what you think is the right thing to say or to do. Write a brief sentence for each question. Write quickly, do not contemplate whether your answers are right or wrong.

    1.   What does financial freedom mean to you?

    2.   What is your earliest memory of wanting to achieve or have money?

    3.   Who are your role models or whom do you admire?

4. What would you like to do, become, or have?

5. What would it take for you to be happy in life?

6. Define happiness for you.

7. Since we were created to be goal striving, achieving human beings, what contribution will you make for the betterment of mankind before you die?

8. Sit down in a quiet place close your eyes and go over the same questions in your mind. And again write whatever comes to mind.

Do you have a dream, or longing, you would like to achieve? How do you decide whether you have a wish/dream or a longing? A wish may or may not happen, because it is placed so far into the future, it is forgotten. Whereas a longing has intensity of feelings and emotions. You think about it more often and replay the scene more frequently in your mind.

To determine your quality/degree of life, answer the following questions to help you diagnose where you are on the continuum of birth to life to death, or life to life cycle.

1. Do you have a dream, or longing, you would like to achieve? What is it?

2. Is this a wish or a longing?

3. What is the difference to you between a wish, dream or longing/goal?

4. How will you decide what you really want out of life?

5. How do/will you decide between conflicting goals/dreams?

6. Has anyone in your family ever set a goal/s to do something, and accomplished it?

7. If your answer to the above is no, how will you develop a desire to achieve, or complete a goal if no one in your family has done the process to make a wish, or dream be a reality?

8. How will you acquire a drive to achieve your goal/s?

9. What aspect of your character will you need to develop that may be dormant or non existent? e.g. achiever, positive outlook, faith, stick-to-ivness, motivation, drive etc.

10. Is amount of money you make your indicator of success? If not what is your indicator of successful completion of a goal/success?

11. Do you feel it is unchristian to desire success, be successful, or have money? Elaborate on this concept.

12. Do you feel money is the "root of all evil," or the evil use of money is the "root of evil"?

13. Have you decided what you really want out of life or is what you want someone else's idea of what would be best for you to do?

14. How long will it take you to complete your goal/s or obtain your desired success?

15. Have you figured out how to start, so your goal becomes real?

    A. What is the first thing you will do to get started? List each step of your plan, from step 1, to step 5. Write down now what you will do and how you will proceed. E.g. decide on a short term goal I can complete in 30 days. These are the thing I will do to make my dream a reality. I will take the following Steps:

1. I will-

2. I will-

3. I will-

4. I will-

B. Now go through the same process for your intermediate goal/s (90 days-1 yr.)
   1. I will-

   2. I will-

   3. I will-

C. Now go through the same process for your long range goal/s (5-10 years).
   1. I will-

   2. I will-

   3. I will-

16. How will you stay focused on your dream/goal?

17. How will you handle a financial setback or disappointment?

God does not cause bad things to happen to us. God works through us by changing our consciousness (mind set), and our heart. God never does anything to us or for us. We create our hardships, disappointments and bad luck through our negative thought patterns and our lack of faith that "God is our refuge and strength, a very present help in trouble."–Psalm 46:1

WORDS OF WISDOM
The great end of life is not knowledge, but action.
–THOMAS HENRY HUXLEY

Chapter 2

Do You Really Want Financial Success?

Do you really want financial success? Wealth is a state of mind. Your thoughts tell who you are and whom you will become. Your financial destiny begins first with your thoughts and your words. Both will bring you closer to the money you desire. To have more money, you must begin by thinking "I can have more and I deserve more". There is a connection between our words and our wealth. To have more money in your life, you will need to change your self-image, and self-respect for yourself and for money. This change must begin first with your thoughts, move to your words, emotions and actions. Your words are the bridge from thought to action. **Rich thoughts lead to rich words and rich words, leads to rich action.** The poorer your thoughts, words and actions, the harder it will be for you to rise above them. The language you use is critical. Always speak the language that shows respect for your self, and for money. For faster results, align your words with your goals. What kind of activity or goal will you undertake to create more wealth.

Great or wealthy people have great dreams, that they put into action which produces the money they desire. What are your financial goals? How much money do you want? Are you totally committed to your dream? What financial goals would you like to achieve, but think is unlikely? Have you given up on you dreams?

Dust Off, those old dreams now. It is time to daydream again. Just as you did when you were a child. Remember when you believed in magic? You thought it, believed it, and it happened. Let's pretend again. It is time to let yourself digress in time to age 5, or 6, the age of magic. Somewhere between the ages of two and nine, magical things seem to happen all the time. Let's take a journey back in time, momentarily in your memory, to a time when you did not have a fear of power, fear of success, fear of failure, fear of identity loss, fear of having too much money or not enough, fear of being different, fear of disapproval, nor a fear of not being liked or accepted.

What happened between the age of nine and your mid-twenties? Who stole your dreams? Who told you that your ideas were foolish, that they could never happen, and even more importantly, you could not accomplish your "far-out" dreams? Was it an overcautious parent, who feared you might experience rejection or ridicule? A shortsighted friend or acquaintance? Did you think that the mind stopped growing with the body? Who taught you how to be so cautious about money? Dreams are the healthy infants, who live inside us, and if properly nurtured with desire and enthusiasm develops into a passion for achievement, and success (personal, social, or financial).

There are many steps along the path to success. If our thoughts are infected with caution and doubt, we get the forerunner of worry to fears. Then we experience fear of achievement, fear of failure, fear of success, low self-esteem and low self-confidence.

Fear inhibits our efforts to achieve our desires and dreams. We want to achieve but, we hear a little voice inside of us that says, "can you do it?" If the answer inside of you says "I'm not sure," more than likely you will never achieve your dream without some guidance to help you move through your own manufactured fears of success. Your dreams eventually fade away and die if they are not fueled with desire or expectation of accomplishment. Without ever knowing why, you begin to feel empty, hollow, lack energy, drive or enthusiasm. If this has happened to you, that is all right. You can start anew today. I hope this book will nudge you to get started, and work through the barriers you have allowed to come between you, and the successful completion of your dreams and goals.

Success means different things to different people. Success

to you may mean losing ten pounds of unwanted weight; to another individual who is a single parent it may mean making enough money to feed and clothe three children. Yet to another woman it may mean making $50,000 a year. While to a home-maker whose children no longer need her, it may signal her transition into the work force for the first time to experience a different kind of success. To a homemaker, success may mean finding a job that will make her feel "needed" again. To a man success may have a different meaning.

What unfulfilled need/wants do you have, that are prodding you to do something different with your life? Why do you want to accomplish something or feel successful? Whatever you define as success, will entail that you take a risk. Success entails you to take risks. It is your ability to get things done, and the right use of your time and resources.

My definition of financial success is the ability and willingness to take risks, to reach your goal, and the ability to handle power in a judicious manner.

Power is the ability to make a decision and follow through with it regardless of the consequences. Power is situational and is relative to the task before you. The kinds of power available to us and the way we use power, will vary depending upon the situation, circumstances, and perceived status of the person involved in the interaction. The key factor in the use of power is to act, or decide without hesitation.

Most women are taught as little girls to defer decision-making to the male of the family. However, this is inconsistent with the assumption of leadership or promoting confidence in one's ability to be the head of household. Often, if the home is a single-parent female household, one of two things may happen. Decisions are made jointly by the female authority figure with outside male input, or decisions are made by the male child with the parent figure relinquishing her power and leadership role in the family to the male child due to a perceived notion that she does not have financial power, or that only men know how to exert power. If the latter occurs, the child gets to have and use power he or she is ill equipped to handle. The child is allowed to assume the role of the adult and misses the opportunity to be a child, and/or to learn from an adult role model effective coping skills to handle life stressors.

Whenever power is placed in the hands of those who are emotionally ill-equipped to use it, the situation is likened to a misguided missile, that becomes dangerous because it wanders aimlessly off its path. If we assume the role and responsibilities of power and leadership authority, we may find ourselves acting child like, and forgetting to take action or we may abdicate our power and leadership role. Also, if we make a blunder in the decision-making process, and are criticized for it, we will grow up with a fear of decision-making and a fear of power because it was associated with a negative outcome.

Many female children see either males making financial decisions and using power or if they see a female using power, the female authority figure is often uncomfortable and unsure of herself and longs for a male partner to assist her in this role.

Most women could benefit from a course in the uses of financial power and decision making. You will need these skills whether you desire success or not. Stop right now, Take a journey within. Then ask yourself, Am I ready for success?

Are you ready for financial success? There are some basic fears you will need to overcome as you embark on your journey for financial success. The first fear is a Fear of Power.

Fear of Power is a major challenge for women, because they have learned to associate power with the male gender rather than the female. Therefore, when many women have a chance to use power, or is in a powerful position they emulate the male behavior, for that position. They fail to modify or feminize their position. So they become confused in their role identity and uncomfortable in their body. Because, there is incongruence between what they are doing and how they perceive themselves. Power is situational. It is always affected by one's gender.

A female in a position of authority does not need to act like a male. If she is secure in her role as an authority figure, she only needs to request or command and if her wishes are not obeyed she needs to have a way to reinforce her commands, and authority so they are carried out by those under her leadership.

Power is not power if one does not have the ability to reinforce one's position of command, or if it is unheeded by those under its command. Most people respect authority and positions of authority. However, there are a few individuals who like to challenge authority figures. If you should ever find yourself in this position, you will need to confront the individual to resolve the matter swiftly and effectively. Otherwise, it can act as a smoldering flame, which if ignored will be to your disadvantage.

Money power not used or misused is just a bad as no power at all. Power must be used in a judicious manner to serve and benefit all parties. The next fear to master is the fear of being different.

Fear of being different. This fear ties closely with a fear of power. To be a woman is to be different, just as it is different to be a man. It is great to be a woman, to be an African-American, to be An A Jewish, Japanese, Chinese, Asian, A Puerto Rican, short, tall, fat, skinny, to speak with an accent, etc. These are qualities that enhance our beauty and individuality. Others will only see these qualities as a problem if you do. Acknowledge that you are different, which is wonderful and get on with the tasks before you.

Fear of not being liked or accepted is a problem only if you allow it to become one. The truth of the matter is that not everyone will like you. Many people hate themselves, so it stands to reason that they will hold you in the same esteem as they do themselves. Just accept that you will not please everyone, and that not all people will like you, for reasons only they know the answer. Just accept it as a fact of life and get on with the business of living your life from integrity and purpose. Seek to get people's respect, not their affection.

If people respect the decision you make, that is enough. The decision you make in their regard may not please them and that is O.K. You are not in a popularity contest to see how many people like or dislike you. You are in your job to reach the company' objectives and get your job done in the most judicious manner possible. Most times it is not what we say but the way in which we say something that creates conflict between us and others.

Most people can handle negative feedback, if it is given in a tactful manner and presented in the form of a sandwich. We sandwich our negative remarks between two positive statements. To try this, give the person one or two positive compliments, then share the negative feedback and remember to conclude with a positive statement. People always remember the last thing we say to them, so be sure to leave them with a positive image of the words you want them to maintain.

Leadership is a lot like fighting on a battle field. Our personal interactions do not always turn out as we would like due to the individuality of others perception of our behavior. Our behavior may be interpreted by others as disapproval or acceptance. We may not always win all of the little battles of life. But, if we can leave others with peace in our minds and heart about our interaction with them commend yourself. For human nature does not always follow a prescribed course of action.

Fear of Disapproval/Rejection is related to the need to be liked. If you received a fair share of disapproval or rejection by a parent figure, you may have a sensitivity towards this and you may wrongly interpret a "no" response and criticism as disapproval or rejection. It is wise not to be overly sensitive. As the saying goes, "Don't wear your heart on your sleeves." It is natural that not all people will agree with the ideas and opinions of all people. Isn't that great? The world would be boring without disagreements.

Fear of Failure. You may ask yourself, what if I fail? So what if you fall down and skin your knee? Do you stay down on the ground? No, you get up, brush yourself off and continue with your business. We must approach success with the same attitude. Success is not always a straightforward path. You may have to zig-zag along the way. You may take a detour. Or, you may stop at any destination along the way and pause. All is O.K. as long as you remember that you paused and know how to get back on track again. If you need a reminder, here it is! You were only supposed to take a short break in your journey to success-fully accomplish your dreams and aspirations. If you have paused too long, it is time now to give yourself a pep talk, reassess the distance before you and work out a road map to suc-cess that is sensible and workable for you. Rest if you must, but never give up on yourself. Tell yourself you can do it. Keep plugging along! And eventually you will reach your destination. PLUG ALONG!

Plug Along

It's the steady, constant driving
To the goal to which you're striving
Not the speed with which you travel,
That will make your victory sure;
It's the everlasting gaining,
Without whimper or complaining
At the burdens you are bearing
Or the woes you must endure.
It's the holding to a purpose,
And never giving in,
It's the cutting down the distance
By the little that you win;
It's the iron will to do it,
And the steady sticking to it.
So what'er your task, go to it!
Keep your grit and plug along!
*—*ANON.

A Treatment For Unexpected Money

I am one with the infinite abundance of God.
I know no separation from life.
I am a divine, perfect expression of the One God, which hav -
ing created all of Life, continually creates Life.
This Creation is working in and through me, Mind acting upon

13

Mind, Life acting upon Life.
It lives through me as perfect activity.
Right now I cease to separate myself from God.
I allow good to come into my experience. I let it flow gener -
ously and abundantly.
There is no great or small in the eyes of God.
I am open to receive.
I am accepting divine Good from an Infinite Source.
I am accepting Abundance. I am expecting to prosper.
I am expecting the unexpected.
I have no concern about paying taxes on this money.
I have no concern about paying tithes.
I put up no barriers.
I am open and receptive to the inflow of Good in my Life.
I thank Thee, Father, Source of all Life.
—REVEREND SHEILA ROBERTS

Fear of Success, never, how could you ever achieve too much, accomplish too much, do or be too much. Most people have the opposite problem. They have not set their heights far enough. They forget to dream and imagine where they could go in their career, or who or what they could become. They see only what is in front of them today, which may be negatively impacted by yesterdays' failures. They forget to set their gaze out into the blue horizons of possibilities to where they could possibly go, do, or become.

The mind needs a visual image reflected upon it through imagining or daydreaming, before it can create a plan to accomplish the things we desire.

No one has ever accomplished a goal, without first visualizing it in their mind and then mapping out a plan to reach their desired goal. Whatever we imagine and ardently desire, we can and will achieve.

If You Can Imagine It, You Can Achieve It,
If You Can Dream It, You Can Become It.
—KRISTONE

There are many books written about visualization. Here is an easy and simple way to utilize visualization techniques to accomplish the things you desire in life. The objective is to use your imagination to conjure a picture in your mind's eye. Go ahead and try this now. This technique will work even if you are not a visual person. First gather all your supplies. You will need a red object. It can be an apple, a red piece of cloth, or an orange object. It can be a shoe, a blouse or a towel. Now let's begin. Become quiet and think about what you want to do. Stare at the red object for approximately 30 seconds. Now close your eyelids. Use your skills of imagery to see if you can picture a visual image of the red object flashing across the screen of your mind. If you can't, continue to practice in this manner until you can see a red object flashing across the screen in your mind's eye. It is O.K. to open your eyes to get a quick peek if the color begins to fade. Do this practice exercise once a day for one week. If you need more time, continue to practice this technique.

After you have mastered this, begin to associate anger, with the red color. Next practice this with the color yellow. Follow the same procedure with the yellow color, except associate the color yellow with the sunshine. Then think of the sunshine and associate the yellow color with happiness.

Now move to the next step of the visualization process. Begin to associate financial success with your new job, promotion, or goals you have outlined for your career. Now get a global picture in your mind's eye about the next step you need to take to move up the career ladder. Now see yourself in a new job position. Become very specific and detailed about what your new job will entail, the location or address of the building, the color of the building and the room.

Imagine the floor in the building where you will be working. Is it on the first floor or the 10th floor over looking the bay? See your name plate with the title on your desk. Imagine the color of the suit you will have on when you go for your interview at the corporation. See the Executive Manager, welcoming you into the firm, telling you that your salary is exactly what you had envisioned. If you leave out any details, go back over this guideline again. Continue daily to do this exercise until every objective you desire is accomplished.

If you are a doubtful person, who tends to imagine the worst outcome of everything, it will take a little longer for you to see positive results. This is a four-stage process.

First, you have to visualize what you want.

Second, you have to believe it can happen.

Third, you have to believe it can happen to you.

Fourth, you must believe you are deserving of this good.

There is a list of books and an audio cassette tape album in the back of this book that you can order to guide you through this process. Be persistent. Know that other people have reached their goals and why not you? Success is not a destination. It is a journey. The journey you will travel, as you achieve your dreams and goals. The following poem summarizes success.

You Must Not Quit

It's all in the state of mind
If you think you are beaten, you are,
If you think you dare not, you don't
If you like to win, but you think you can't
It is almost certain you won't.
If you think you'll lose, you're lost,
For out in the world we find
Success begins with a fellow's will—
It's all in the state of mind.
If you think you are outclassed, you are,
You've got to be sure of yourself before
You can ever win a prize.
Life's battles don't always go
To the stronger or faster man,
But soon or late the person who wins
Is the person who thinks they can!
—ANON

You are where you are today because of the thoughts you think, moment by moment, mental image (visualization) you hold about you/your life, expectations you/others have about your ability, and the vision you entertain about your life's purpose. Reverend Michael Beckwith says, "visioning is different from visualization; it is a transformation of the human self, into the divine, spiritual self to allow the presence of God to use you." And you do not tell God what to do, nor ask God for anything. You glorify God, by allowing God to express through you, for a "Higher" purpose to serve your fellow man. I suggest you start with visualization, to train your mind to expect better, a higher good, to achieve your goals. Then shift to the visioning process, as outlined by Michael Beckwith, where you become a master like the great mystics. And allow the universe to use you, by aligning yourself with divine ideas of joy, harmony, love, and wisdom. To do this you will need self-awareness.

Self-Awareness — Is the ability to see yourself as you really are, to accurately assess your own needs, your strong and weak points and areas in which you need to improve. It is easy to think that we are perfect and everyone else needs to improve. We can all become better people. Periodically make out a personal growth chart for yourself, grade yourself on a scale of one to ten. Some of the categories might be "quick temper," "easy going," "hard driver," "relaxed," "cooperative," "stubborn." Do this annually to gauge how much growth you have achieved. For greater effectiveness and to increase your self-awareness have a co-worker and a friend grade you. Then compare the score you gave yourself to the score that each of them gave you.

Salesmanship — All successful entrepreneurs need a course in salesmanship. All of life is about selling. You will need to sell someone on the idea, you are the best person for the job, and that they need to hire you. You may need to sell the people working under you or over you on a new idea you would like to put into effect. You may need to sell your boss on the idea that you deserve a promotion or a salary increase. Do take a class in selling. If nothing else you will learn how to sell you on you.

MONEY

You are a product, and you are a commodity. You have skills and talents. You have value. Will you be undersold? Who will decide how much you are worth?

To move to the top of the financial ladder you will need to sell your services and talents and no one knows how valuable you are, but you. Are you worth the effort and time someone would need to pay if they hired you? If you cannot resoundingly say yes to these questions, begin to work on your self-esteem. Seek the assistance of professionals who can help you. Be willing to pay to become a better product (person). Be realistic and honest with yourself. Seek ways to improve yourself. You are a commodity. Are you a Volkswagen or Mercedes Benz? It's all a state of mind. The mind is the creative cause of all that transpires in a person's life. Our personal conditions are the results of our actions and our actions are the results of the thoughts and ideas we think.

A Drive to Action — This is where you pull together all of the above traits and characteristics into concrete, realistic, effective action. Whereby you take advantage of the opportunities afforded you and transcend the obstacles before you.

Life in its great and wonderful abundance is pouring itself out to us as unexpected good, in the form of unexpected money.

Affirm by stating out loud, "I now claim for myself unexpected money."

The greatest thing about man is his ability to transcend
himself, his ancestry, and his environmnent, to
become what he dreams.
–Tully C. Knoles

Chapter 3

Are You Ready for Money?

The exercises in this section will help you to decide what is your mission in life. It will allow you to assess how far you have come in this process and help you determine if you have the character traits and skills needed to achieve your goal/s. It will teach you how to focus and stay focused so that you can stay motivated with your chosen vision. It will help you to make sense out of all the mumble, jumble, chatter in your mind. You will learn the principles of success and will be able to decide by the end of the quiz if you are a candidate for success.

Self Test

Are You Ready for Business Success

1. I know what I want out of life? Yes □ / No □
2. Have I chosen a business that blends with my personality, abilities and interests? Yes □ / No □
3. I know my business strengths and weaknesses and I have taken measures to utilize the services and skills of others to balance my weaknesses. Yes □ / No □
4. I have accepted that I will need the services of competent professional for my business growth and I am prepared to pay for these services. Yes □ / No □
5. Do you have financial and quantitative goals set for you and your business? Yes □ / No □
6. Do you have an action plan for accomplishing your goals and are they tied to a time frame? Yes □ / No □
7. Are you self-disciplined? Yes □ / No □
8. Can you work long hours and make sacrifices? Yes □ / No □
9. Do you have management ability? Yes □ / No □

10. Do you have enough experience in your field?
    Yes ☐ / No ☐
11. Are your goals realistic and obtainable? Yes ☐ / No ☐
12. Do you love what you do? Yes ☐ / No ☐
13. Is your purpose to own a business clear to you?
    Yes ☐ / No ☐
14. Do you love how money can serve humanity, or you
    obsessed with hoarding money? Yes ☐ / No ☐

Dr. Dorothy Height, president of the National Council of Negro Women when asked, "what makes the great?" stated "Greatness is not measured by what a man or woman accomplishes, but by the opposition he or she overcame to reach their goals."

You can be a success in any business you desire. The Reverend Johnnie Coleman, Pastor of the Christ Universal Complex in Chicago teaches, "You don't have to be sick or broke. You can go within and bring forth the power to change things." Each of us has within us a sleeping giant, which when activated with desire, a strong determination, and unrelenting persistence will eventually melt away the greatest obstacles in our path. Success, whether business or otherwise belongs to the person who will pursue what they desire tenaciously without giving in to despair, set backs, disappointment, tragedy or failure. They achieve success because they never look back with regret at the past, but continue to look ahead to the possibilities of the future. These people have an unshakable faith, and belief in a God that is ready, willing, able to take care of them, and sustain them through their trials and tribulations.

According to Dr. Hugh Gloster, the past president of Morehouse College, when asked "what made him one of America's one hundred best college presidents?' Replied "You must establish your dreams and quietly move in the direction of attaining them." Much of this has to do with the way we use our mind. In the books, "Working With The Law," by Raymond Holliwell and "Think And Grow Rich, A Black Choice," by Dennis Kimbro and Napoleon Hill, both authors discuss mental laws and how the use of them can create wealth.

Everything you see now began as an idea in someone's mind. Your physical world is nothing more than the lingering evidence of that which has already taken place in your mind. It is an extension or out picturing of your thoughts. Yours is a mental world. Raymond Holliwell states, "mental laws are the infrastructures of life." Kimbro states, "Just as one is blinded to physical laws, mental laws are also undetectable to the eye." Thoughts and ideas are living, breathing, things. They are the raw materials from which all we desire, create, or accomplish in life comes from.

Therefore, right now you are where you are in your business or financial condition because of the thoughts you are thinking. If you desire a change in your business or in your finances, you must examine the quality of thoughts you entertain on an hourly basis. The more you think about lack, bad times, or scarcity, the more these circumstances will appear in your life. William James, the Harvard Psychologist stated "You are what you think about most of the time." What you think on increases and grows in proportion to the amount of energy thought you feed it. Therefore, if you desire success or wealth, make this your predominant thought for twenty-two hours in a twenty-four-hour day.

To have money or acquire money will require that you increase your prosperity consciousness. And here are some principles that can help you. **First, *prosperity is a state of mind. As you think, you become.* Second, *prosperity is a state of mind that results from right thinking.*** It is the result of your recognition of the nature of your inner being. Your inner self is a creative individual expression of God. Because the nature of God is abundant, and prosperous, when you identify your human nature with your God nature, you see yourself as a child of God. An individualized, creative, expression of God. You were made in the image and likeness of God. Also you came from God and after your stay on earth you return to God. You are the vessel through which God manifest and express. The nature of God is: Joy, Love Prosperity, Abundance, Wholeness, Perfection,

Competence, and Justice. You are one with God, so you are all of these as well.

You are not lacking in any physical trait or character for the perfection, prosperity, abundance, and wholeness, of God to come forth through you. What is needed is a correction or realignment in your thinking or thought patterns. You need to make a shift in your mind from lack to abundance, from help-lessness to being hopeful, from an impoverished outlook to a prosperous outlook. Learn to think optimistic, positive and upbeat thoughts. Have an unwavering faith in God's ability to provide for your needs. If God can provide for the birds of the air, the fish in the sea, and the worms of the earth, surely God must love you enough to provide for you. God has not abandoned you.

Maybe, it is you who have abandoned God, rather than God abandoning you. You have to pray to heal your mind of a belief in fear, lack, or limitation. You must keep your mind on God and the Goodness of God, on a continuous and daily basis. Prosperity is an inner spiritual state of adequacy, abundance, fullness, love, joy, harmony, peace, and forgiveness from harm, or wrong by you or others.

The two emotional states, that prepare you to be prosperous, is gratitude and forgiveness. Affirm daily that your every need is known by God, and supplied before you ask, because God loves you, and knows what you need before you ask. You were not sent to earth to fend for yourself. You are God's child, and God will take care of HIS children. You come through your parents, Physically. They are your human nurturer and protector, but spiritually you belong to God.

Whatever you become in life is the result of your sustained energy and focus over a long period of time. This explains why success is not a straight path. Most of us have a lot of negative mental conditioning and programming that has to be unlearned. This process of change can be likened to having a bucket of dirty water that you want to become clear water. If you replace the dirty water with a bucket full, it will get clear more quickly than if you replace the water with a spoon. However, the rate of change will be proportional to your willingness to give up your old negative thought patterns, your comfortable ways of doing things; to learn a new way of being. And be open to change and grow on a daily or hourly basis. There are many personal and professional success skills you will need to develop, before you achieve proficiency in your new endeavor.

Affirm The Perfect Expression Of Abundance

Prosperity is the nature of perfect Being. Prosperity is a state of mind. Therefore as I think, I become. Prosperity is a state of being that comes from right thinking and can only result from my recognition of the nature of my inner being. I am meant to be successful. My freedom as a creative individualization of God enables me to achieve success in every phase of life. This state of freedom is true spiritual prosperity. Prosperity, received and established in my mind, is automatically manifested in my world.

I have the ability to be my complete, creative, best self at all times, under any circumstance. Prosperity results from my desire and intention to express God in me.

There can be no limit to my prosperity, because God removes all limitation from my consciousness. As I am freed from the bondage of my fears and false beliefs, I experience true manifestation of prayer. My spiritual nature brings me real prosperity. From the center of my inner being all abundance works come forth. I identify myself with the abundance of God, and I am prosperous today.

Today I claim my affluence, abundance, and prosperity. I experience fullness. I claim my good and go where I want to go and do what I want to do as long as it does not interfere with others. I affirm my prosperity. I receive and use money, knowing that it indicates spiritual prosperity. I have freedom, and God is expressed fully in me when I am free.

Through my word, I make known to the abundant universe what I want. I individualize the Universal. Whatever I ask, I receive.

MONEY

Biblical Quotes For Prosperity

Let the Lord be magnified, which hath pleasure
in the prosperity of His servant.
–PSALM 35:27

Thou open thine hand, and satisfiest the desire
of every living thing.
–PSALM 145:16

I Live the Fullness of Life, Now

It is a deep satisfaction to be alive today. I am glad I know who I am and what I am. I am a child of God. It is satisfying to know that everything I do is the action of God within me. I experience the full gratification of every desire, when I make my will one with the Universal will. God working within me satisfies my every demand on the eternal law of perfect self expression. I live at the point of cause, and the effect is complete fulfillment. My life is the Father's life and is an outlet for his creativity to express through me. I am the focal point in the universal creative mind of God. I am a willing servant, and open vessel for the Goodness of God to flow through, and so it is.

Chapter 4

How To Survive
In The Business World

The way to the top is much like a journey or a hunting trip. You may make many detours and it may seem at times that you have lost your way. Take heart, the detour may turn out to be missing information you need to complete your expedition.

Pay attention to your intuition and hunches along the way, for they will seldom lead you astray. Our mind is always working to help us realize our dream and desires. If you say to yourself, I need to learn to be more subtle, your mind will find a way to accommodate you. The mind is always working to help us achieve our desires. You may think to yourself, "I wouldn't want to work for a strict boss," Your mind hears, "strict boss," and it begin to look for ways to give you your desire. A year later you may find yourself working under an autocratic executive in a large corporation.

If you are an aggressive, cutthroat type of person, you will need to learn subtlety. The mind works to accommodate us, so it will provide an opportunity for you to learn how to be more subtle. However, learning a new skill is not easy. It may be very stressful for you, so you may decide to seek employment elsewhere; and that is okay. The road to the top of the corporate ladder is not always a straight one. What if you have to detour along the way? The valuable skills you develop will provide you a solid foundation. And the detour can act as a leverage to move you to the next rung of the ladder. Money is one of the key commodities you will need to move your business forward.

Patience is an important trait you will need throughout your career. Patience with yourself and others.

Do not become wary, and disappointed with yourself if you

are not moving as swiftly as you had envisioned. For you could be gathering valuable information that can assist you later in your climb up the corporate ladder.

As you move along your career path. Do a periodic assessment of your goals. Noting where you want to go and what steps, you need to take to reach your objectives. Do this once a year, preferably at the beginning of the year.

Make this one of your New Year's resolutions. Sit down; take out a 8½ x 11 sheet of paper, turn it so the lines are vertical rather than horizontal and make 3 columns: Skills I possess, Skills I need to possess, Skills necessary for me to have to reach my desired goal. Be honest and truthful with yourself. If you feel you are too aggressive or passive, take an assertiveness class. Then you will have an objective assessment database from which to glean information.

Continue to look at ways you can improve your personal competence. See yourself as a piece of equipment. Are you an upgraded piece of equipment, or are you an outdated piece of equipment? Remember your employer is looking for value, not a warm body. Just, how valuable are you to the corporation? Have you taken a course lately to stay abreast of the newer technologies in your field? Can you be placed in more than one work environment within the corporation? Just how valuable are you? If you have limited skills, either professionally or personally you will soon be replaced. You will be replaced with a more skillful person.

How valuable you make yourself to the corporation determines how far you go up the corporate ladder. Even in companies where nepotism is practiced. If you show the corporation or top management how you can assist them in reaching their goals, a nitch will be created for you. It is wise to have some basic knowledge about how corporations are structured and how they function. You need to know the rules to play the game.

All organizations are divided into two major structures: **Formal and Informal**. The *formal structure* of a company is composed of all the official policies, rules, job titles, etc., that are designed to make the company work. The informal structure, is composed of the friendship and association networks that unofficially make the organization function. For example, if you look for a job through the formal structure of an organization, you send a resume to the personnel manager. If you looking for a job through the informal structure of an organization, you call a friend in the organization who calls her/his buddy in the department of your choice, who talks to the boss, who calls you. Occasionally this can happen.

Every organization creates a formal structure which is intended to fulfill the goals of the organization. The formal structure is all the rules, policies, procedures, official job duties and division of labor created by the top management to fulfill organizational objectives. The ultimate purpose of every formal structure is to provide quality service or product and therefore, make money.

Formal Power and Influence: Businesses are generally divided into two divisions of labor, the staff and line. The staff (or support functions) usually includes all administrative positions: Examples are personnel, purchasing, accounting (payables and receivables) and training. Line personnel handle jobs which are directly involved with income production for the company. In a retail organization, line personnel include sales people and store managers. In hospitals, they are doctors and nurses. In manufacturing organizations, line personnel include factory workers and engineers or product designers.

Chain of Command and Protocol: According to Natasha Josefowitz, 1980, there are basically three levels of power in the chain of command continuum; *dependent power, intermediate power,* and *influence power*. People at the lowest rung on the ladder have dependent power. They have entry-level jobs which provide them with little control over their work situation. Also, they have little or no decision-making responsibility and a very narrow range of duties.

People with *intermediate power* have some decision-making responsibility and influence over others; but they are under the influence of higher-ups. Supervisors, managers, and senior professional staff are examples of middle-level positions.

Influence power, these positions are at the top of the chain of command. Examples of people with influence power are the President, Vice President, the Director, the Dean of the College, and the Hospital Administrator. The decisions these people make have the broadest impact on the organization.

Now that you have a working knowledge about the structure of an organization, remember you are a key member; what you do can impact your career as you move up the corporate ladder.

You are an asset to the corporation. To get promoted, you need tangible and marketable skills that will assist the corporation in expanding.

Skills you will need to survive in the corporate world are:
1. Speaking skills
2. Presentation skills
3. Positive self-esteem
4. Desire for challenge
5. Creativity
6. Desire for power
7. Negotiation skills
8. Ability to delegate
9. Independence
10. Ability to Balance Empathy and Objectivity
11. Desire for change
12. Desire for competition
13. Opportunism
14. Wisdom

Speaking skills — You will need to have mastery over your ability to express your ideas and opinions in a logical, orderly manner. You will need to be able to think quickly, and speak to the issue when called upon, at a moments notice. A cost effective simplistic training program is a toastmistress or toastmaster group. For the club listing in your locality, check the phone directory or contact your local Chamber of Commerce.

Presentation skills — This is a threefold process. We present ourselves through the way we speak, dress and interact with other people. It would be a good idea for you to attend one of the free wardrobe shows given by one of the local department stores. Call to ask when and if such event is being offered. If you are unable to attend a free session, it would be worth your money to have a color analysis done by a professional, to ascertain which color=s best bring out your skin tone coloring. What is your body-type frame, and the best style clothing to wear to emphasize or de-emphasize certain body proportions?

If you wish to be successful, it is worth your time to give the right impression. What you choose to wear says something about how you wish to be seen. Your attire does not need to be expensive. It needs to be clean, neat, simple, and in good taste. Avoid wearing clothes that make you stand out. Let people notice you and your talents rather than your clothing. A suit or dress with a jacket is always in good taste. It is wise to have a gray or blue suit in your wardrobe, additionally for females a beige, black or white dress. For men, black shoes are always in style. Women may want to have a pair of beige and navy blue shoes in their possession.

Everything you say is judged on two levels: *What you say and the way you deliver it.* Many people put themselves down by the words they use. The use of qualifying statements before you speak diminishes the impact of your message and also affects the impression others will have of you. Examples of this are: starting a sentence with, "May I say something," does not encourage people to listen. Other sentence prefaces are "I don't know," "Maybe I should," "I kind of." Examples of the use of superlatives are "terrific," "fantastic," "great," all detract from your presence.

It would help you to secure the services of a voice or theatrical coach who has access to video feedback so you can see and hear how you come across to others as you present yourself. Again in many toastmasters club, this is sometimes available for free, but the feedback may not be as detailed as you might like.

MONEY

If finances are a consideration for you. You can tape record a message and play it back, to critique yourself. Also, you can give a presentation standing in front of the mirror. Pay close attention to your body posture, i.e., the way you hold your head to one side, raise one shoulder, body rigidity and breathing pattern.

Ask several friends or two different neighbors to critique your presentation, and to give you objective feedback. Tell them you want the truth, even if it is unpleasant. You might write out a list of things you want them to check off, to make it easier for them in their critique of you. Some people have trouble saying unpleasant things—when asked for an opinion.

Positive Self-Esteem — I cannot say enough about positive self-esteem. You will either fail or go to great heights in your career, depending upon your measure of a positive self-image. A positive self-image lays the foundation for our positive self-esteem. Our self-esteem is the foundation for self-mastery. Self-mastery is a life long process, it is an accumulation of all the thoughts we have held throughout our life. The words we speak to ourselves and others are expressions of our thoughts and beliefs. To have self-mastery, we must look at what we think about, most of the time and what we believe.

Who you are today, is an accumulation of what you have, told yourself, and the beliefs you formed as a result of your inner dialogue. We shape our life by the choices we make, which are influenced by the thoughts we accept, or reject.

> *"For by thy words thou shall be justified, and by*
> *thy words thou shall be condemned,"*
> –MATTHEW 12:37, KING JAMES BIBLE.

If you have a good opinion of yourself, it can be eroded by having negative people around you. We influence and are influenced by the people with whom we associate. The key is a high self-esteem level. It is wise to take a refresher course to keep your level of self-esteem high. Read other books by the author: Soft Power Negotiation Skills™, Light the Fire Within You.

How To Improve Self-Esteem In The African American Child, Self-Esteem The Essence of You, and How To be A Success In Business. In the back of this book is an audio cassette tape album you can order to help you maintain your positive self-esteem.

Mental imagery and visualization can be used, to help you create the job position you desire. To do this, find a quiet spot in your home. Turn off the radio and T.V., put on loose, comfortable clothing. Sit, take in a couple of deep breaths, then exhale slowly, and repeat the process again. Imagine yourself being in a calm peaceful and relaxing place, then bring to mind the job position you desire. See, in your imagination the location, (street, building, floor) be as specific as you can with the details. See yourself at your desk. Visualize the dress or suit you will be wearing and the title on your desk. Be sure to visualize your interview with your future boss. See him welcoming you and introducing you to the people who will be working for you. Visualize the salary you desire, flashing the figures across your mind's eye in bold, bright green colors. Money is green, so see lots of fresh green dollar bills. Do this exercise once a day. Just before you go to bed for 30 days, then once a week for 30 days. Repeat this process until you get the job position you are desiring.

Remember to sell yourself at every available opportunity. Your boss needs to know about the great things you have done, or are doing. However, be discreet and use tact. Right timing is very important when you are selling another person on yourself. The purpose of this exercise is to allow your imagination to brainstorm your environmental preferences. For a moment, allow yourself to create the perfect work environment for you.

Creative Visualization
Describe your environment (structure, office, outdoors/indoors, colors used, type of decor, furniture, location, etc.)

MONEY

How would you be dressed?

How many people will you be working with, and how does your work interface with theirs?

Where do you fit into the work hierarchy?

What attitudes are encouraged and rewarded?

What strengths will you bring with you?

What would you be saying to yourself about your new career?

Desire for challenge — You will need a compelling reason or reasons to inspire you onward with your career. Therefore, write out your goals. Keep them in view, so that you can see them often. What is your challenge? Is it to move to a better neighborhood? Get new braces for your child's teeth? Install a swimming pool or a Jacuzzi in your back yard? Get a weekly pedicure, manicure and facial? Make $50,000 a year? Become the first female corporate executive in your firm? For a man, it may be an additional $100,000 to pay for college expenses. You need a desire for challenge. A burning desire to achieve, that will inspire you to want to move up the corporate ladder. If you have not given this much thought, take the time now to decide what you want in life.

What challenge or challenges would you like to overcome? Give yourself a time frame (one year, two years etc.). When do you plan to accomplish your goal? Remember to set realistic goals. You may need to enroll in adult education classes, attend jr. college or a university to acquire the necessary skills, for the job you desire. Maybe you will be the first person in your family to graduate from college. Do you have a strong enough reason, that will propel you, to move up the corporate ladder?

Creativity — I define creativity as *risk taking behavior, without fear, utilizing problem solving skills.* You will need to be very creative to know when to make the right moves that will move you forward on your career path.

Risk taking behaviors require that you use every bit of your ingenuity and creativity. It requires determination and effort. **Here are some of the areas you may encounter:**

1. Male dominated company that uses "old boy standards" to move up in the corporation. You are a female; you are stuck at a certain level and can't seem to get promoted. Do you file a grievance with the labor relations department? Do you file a grievance with the Equal Employment Opportunity Commission, or do you try to get a good evaluation and seek employment at a more progressive firm? How you respond will have a lot to do with your goals. Are you a female trying to change company policies of discrimination towards females? If your goal is to move ahead as swift as possible, you may not want to make waves. Even if you transfer out of the corporation, how do you know if you will receive a favorable recommendation? You may be given a formal letter of recommendation to take with you, and have an unfavorable phone call precede you. You will need to use your creative abilities to ascertain what course of action to take.

2. Do you know the rules of your corporation? *What are*

the office politics? Do you have to play politics to move up in the corporation? What have others before you did to get promoted? Are there cliques in the organization? Do you need to be a part of one? If so, which one leads to advancement? How have other females advanced in the corporation? Is it necessary to have a non-business relationship with the boss to get promoted? It is wise to learn early what the formal and informal rules of the corporation are. Until you do, it is better to maintain detachment from all groups, until you know which is the "in group" (movers) and which is the "out group" (the watchers and gossiper). You may not want to become bosom buddies with the gossiper but you might want to listen in, to find out about the office politics and in-house happenings.

3. *Luncheon, business meeting, social engagement; you are new on the job!* You are invited by your boss to all of the above. Should you accept all three invitations or decline all three. Until you know the rules of the corporation, you are safer attending a business meeting where the matters to be discussed will follow corporate protocol and thereby dictate how you and others will interact. Always keep before you your goals, you are there to move up the corporate ladder, not seek a husband or wife. If to seek a lover or mate is one of your goals, it is a good business practice to keep the two separate. It reduces the risk of emotional abuse for both parties.

4. *Help the boss look good* — remember your first loyalty is to the corporation. Your goal is to help the corporation profit. If you present professional, ethical demeanor, you will be perceived that way and treated in that manner. However, as a female if you are at a social function and the boss makes an off-colored remark to you, you may have to take a risk, by telling him you are offended by the remark. The same applies for a male with a female boss. It is better to look at yourself in the

mirror than to have your boss assume you like to be treated with disrespect. Right timing is the key here. If your boss was inebriated when he/she made the remark, you might want to wait, when he/she is sober speak with him/her.

Let them know that you respect them, but you felt disrespect by the comment/s made by him/her. Say you like to treat others with respect and you like for others to treat you with respect.

Whenever you are in a *social gathering* and someone makes a disrespectful comment to you, *do not* join in the laughter, move away quickly to show your disapproval.

Whenever you engage in risk taking behavior without fear, it shows that you know how to use power and that you are not afraid of it.

Desire for power — To move up the corporate ladder you will need to have a healthy desire for power. *Power is the ability to get people to do what you want them to do, and the ability to avoid being forced to do what you don't want to do.* Some key guidelines to know about power are:

1. **Build relationships** — gratitude and obligation can give you power leverage. Make sure the people working under you have a positive impression of you. They are more likely to trust you and want to do as you suggest.

   Regardless of your position within an organization, you need to be aware of protocol. Bosses generally want to know who's doing what, when, and with whom. They never want to find out information through a second source. The key is to always keep your boss informed of your activities. Periodically update your superior; this gives you an opportunity to share some of the good things you are doing, make a request, or get feedback about your opportunities for advancement.

2. Your power base increases as the number of people dependent on you increases. How many people need your knowledge or input?

3. **Establish credibility** — stand behind what you say and do. Keep your word and follow through on your promises.

4. **Become an expert** — Develop a reputation as an expert, this way others will come to rely on you and defer to your judgment.

5. **Data control** — Control as much as possible the flow of information. To have privileged information that others desire can increase your power base immensely.

6. **Personal Control** — What resources are you able to control? The major ones are money, employees, equipment etc.

7. **Be interested in other people** — know how people feel about important issues; seek to win their respect.

8. **Know the sources of power** — Observe and listen to the grapevine. Who are the movers in the organization? Who is quoted most often? Pay attention to these tidbits of information.

    Observe what gets rewarded and what receives disapproval. Notice what happens if deadlines are not met or procedures are not followed? If possible, try to find out why the boss seems to dislike someone or why someone was let go. All of this is valuable information that can aid you in your climb to the top of the corporation. Observe symbols of power and who has them: Symbols of power are any visible benefits which are offered to employees above a certain level example, company cars, choice parking spots, an office facing the ocean etc. Often these benefits are given to an employee who is on the way up the corporate ladder.

9. **Be willing to take a risk** — Be willing to risk the power you have to obtain more. There are no hard rules to follow, as when to take a risk, and when not to. But

if you rely on your intuition, you will seldom go wrong. Remember, if you get fired it is not the end of the world. Sometimes you need to let go of something, to discover what you don't want.

10. **Avoid losing power** — Sidestep activities and projects that could have an adverse effect on the power you have.

11. **Be ethical** — Don't lie, cheat or break your promise.

12. **How to use power positively to impact the lives of others** — If you are in charge of memos, meetings, agendas or schedules, others will need your approval. This will place you in a position of power.

13. **Be aware of how your actions are viewed by others** — Are you seen as supporting others, or do you have a label as a self-serving individual?

14. **Employees** — The greater your responsibilities, the more you need to rely on the cooperation and help of others. Unless the people working under you is loyal, they may not follow your orders. Seek to establish a trusting and bonding alliances of a few key people to leverage your power base?

Remember, power is about forming and maintaining dependent and interdependent relationships with persons under your leadership. It can be good or bad, constructive or destructive. The choice is yours.

Whoever becomes great, must render great service. Likewise, whoever finds themselves at the top must lose themselves at the bottom. Meaning, you will need to trade your old self-image for a newer self-image that matches your title.

Also, everyone who is now at the top was once at the bottom. They had to create success for themselves and learn to accept their success image.

Your ability to negotiate and use power wisely will critically influence the outcome of your success. The use of Soft Power™ negotiation skills, will enable you to negotiate with others to get what you want, and still have harmonious relations with them.

MONEY

All successful people in positions of authority know how to negotiate, and their negotiation skills are an asset to them and the organization they serve. These are the factors involved in effective negotiation skills.

Negotiation Skills — Factors involved in negotiation are:
1. **Communication** — Listen and act on what we hear. To send and receive information with understanding.
2. **Relationship** — Personal/Impersonal. You will need to maintain a degree of detachment whether you are dealing with a friend, family member, or business associate.
3. **Attitude** — Positive/Negative. Others tend to mirror our attitude and behavior. Be positive in outlook if you want a positive outcome.
3. **Self-Image** — Self-Worth, deserving. Project the image you want and deserve to have your needs met.
4. **Self-Esteem** — Right to have one's basic needs met; to esteem and accept oneself as valuable.
5. **Life Position** — Powerful/powerless; choice/no choice; independent/dependent; control/no control.
6. **Self-Confidence** — Courage to ask for what you want, expecting to get it; belief in oneself.
7. **Creativity** — Ability to use your ingenuity in problem solving situation.
8. **Orientation to Life** — Personality style/conflict resolution style. The way you interact with others is indicative of your learned coping patterns to handle frustration, conflict, anger, and criticism.

Negotiation is a process which occurs any time we attempt to influence the behavior of another so as to cause them to comply with our wishes and desires. It implies that a *desire* demands satisfaction and a *need* is unfulfilled.

Ability to delegate — The ability to delegate is a skill worth developing in you. As you move up the corporate ladder and assume more responsibilities, you will need the assistance of others to maximize your time, effort and resources.

Foremost of all, *decide what tasks you will delegate and*

which you will do yourself. Once you delegate, let the individuals know up front that you may need to make corrections as you go along and that you will need input from them; also tell them that you will need to have periodic reviews to gauge the success of the project/tasks. This way they will be expecting to be accountable to you for their work activities. If you lay out the ground rules before hand, they are less likely to view you as meddling when you inquire about their activities later. You might want to agree on an acceptable review conference schedule. If the project before you has a time deadline, you may need to have a weekly or monthly review. Here are some points to keep in mind as you decide what to delegate to whom:

1. **The buck stops with you.** You will be held accountable whether the project fails or succeed. You will lose the loyalty of your subordinates if they are blamed for the failure. Also your superiors will not respect you if you place the blame on your subordinates. Just admit that the situation did not turn out as you expected.

2. **Know what to delegate.** If you have been asked to handle the task, don't delegate it. They want your expertise. Even though the task may be very simple. Someone respects your abilities. Be glad.

3. **Be selective.** Delegate the right task to the right person. Try to match the skills of the task to the person. You will be less likely to hear complaints and you will be pleased to know that the job is in competent hands.

4. **Be explicit.** Make certain your delegates understand what they are to do. Have well-defined goals. Ask for clarification and feedback. If they can state back to you, the overall concept of what you said you have obtained your objective.

5. **Responsibility.** Try to foster a sense of responsibility in your delegates. Let them know you are counting on them to do well.

6. **Authority.** Define the limits of authority they will have. Let them know that the authority may be shared

between you and them. However, if at all possible assign them total responsibility for minor job tasks. Let them know that they need to check with you if ever they are doubtful about overstepping their boundaries.

7. **Decision-making.** Plan on making the big decisions yourself and let them analyze, advise and recommend.

8. **Independent action.** Encourage independence. Allow your delegates to act, without checking with you before their every move. This will help them feel that you have confidence in them. Also it will help them to feel more competent in what they are doing. Focus more on "what" they do, rather than "how" they carry out your instructions.

9. **Expect excellence**. Set the example, expect high standards of workmanship from both yourself and those working under you. Let them know in advance that you want quality workmanship. Think of ways you can reinforce this behavior through some form of positive reinforcement.

10. **Rewards**. People will not work for long without some form of reward. Be supportive. Try to operate more as a team leader. Encourage and coach rather than dictate. Encourage them to succeed. Let them and others above you, know when they have done a good job. This will bolster their morale, and motivate them to work harder to be a good team member.

    Know when things have run off track. Make necessary corrections when needed. If negative feedback is needed, use the sandwich approach. State two positive factors, give the negative corrective feedback, then end with a positive statement. Let them know they are still an important part of the team. Take every opportunity to build up their morale and they will in turn do the same for you.

11. **Build trust and respect**. Strive for mutual trust and respect from those working under your leadership. Take

the necessary time to build an atmosphere of trust, respect, cooperation and open communication. This may take some time, but the long term benefits are worth it to you.

If this is your first time having subordinates work under you, be understanding. Don't place the whole work load on them at once, share part of the work load. It will help them to see you as a caring superior. It will make them work even harder to support you and your goals. The ability to delegate is an art and will take time and practice. Be a good team manager. Working as a team manager allows you to demonstrate independent leadership.

12. **Independence** — To move up the corporate ladder you will need to show that you are a leader. Leaders do not need group approval or reinforcement to bolster their self-esteem. They tend to view groups as a means of sharing ideas, information and problem solving.

All corporate executives have to be willing to take risks to advance their careers. Risk taking means to act, in hope, that the outcome is favorable. If you have a fear of failure or are uncertain, you may want to be more pragmatic and avoid taking big risks. Confront your fears and act when you think it wise. Rely on your intuition to guide you.

Always have a clear idea of how much power and authority you have. Know your limitations. Use wisdom and good judgment. There will be times when you should not act. Rely on your intuitions to guide you.

Ability to Balance Empathy and Objectivity. — It is wiser to access any situation before you act. You want to take care that your objectivity is not hampered by your feelings. As a supervisor, you will need to play many roles; you need to be able to move in and out of a role quickly and gracefully. You can be empathetic to the needs of others and still maintain objectivity; the key is detachment. View yourself as a judge who is giving an impartial decision; this way you can maintain a healthy balance between empathy and objectivity. Know your limitations and be honest with yourself. There is times when you may need to side step a situation because your objectivity is clouded by personal experiences.

Desire for change. — Do not be fearful if you are fired. Being fired maybe the best thing that could happen to your career. You may have reached a plateau in your former job. A variety of experiences can be critical to the advancement of your career.

The path to the top of the corporate ladder is not always straight. You may need to move horizontally or diagonally to advance your career. Move to another if it is to your advantage.

If you can get free training in high technology or computer training, take it. You may have to start on a lower entry pay level, but the ability to advance within the corporation may be excellent.

Be willing to take a risk. *Comfort is not always growth*. You may be very comfortable in your present job environment, but how far will you have advanced in ten years? Will you be making the $70,000 you had set out to make within 10 years if that is your goal? Always maintain a competitive edge for yourself.

Desire for competition

You will need a strong, healthy desire for competition to move up the corporate ladder. There may be times when the odds are against you. However, if you have a strong drive to achieve, you can overcome the tendency to become discouraged or wanting to quit. This is the time when a strong faith in a power greater than you can provide the courage to hang in there. A strong faith in God assures you that you are not alone. One of my favorite bible quotations to use as a "pick me up," is *Greater is He that is within you, than he that is in the world.*

Be willing to take a risk to advance your career. Plan before hand to have a contingency plan in case things do not turn out as you had planned. Be willing to compromise or negotiate if necessary. Try to gauge in advance how far you can go before you reach a point of no return. *Know when to push and when to pull. Also know when to quit.* Don't be discouraged if you risk and lose. Nothing ventured—nothing gained. Most people who achieve greatness have failed. They were able to learn from their failure and became strategically better the second, or third time around.

Opportunism. — To succeed in Corporate America you will need to be an opportunistic entrepreneur. Each day you live, you tread on uncharted terrain. Keep a keen eye. Be forever looking out for new opportunities; when you see one, seize it. It may not come back again. Keep an open mind. Be kind, cordial and considerate to all people regardless of the sex, race or creed. The person you help may be the one to aid you after a devastating blow to your career. Pause often to count your gains and your losses. Whatever you do, do it with style and class. Do it with gusto, heart, vim and vigor. If you are a leader act like a leader. Remember, all good leaders know how to follow when necessary. Aim high, but know how to fall to grace.

The path to the top of the corporate ladder is often arduous, rugged, and stormy. Stop, often, along the way to smell the roses and enjoy the scenery on your way to the top. As you move up the corporate world take the prayer of serenity with you.

The Serenity Prayer
God, Grant me the serenity to accept
the things I cannot change,
The courage to change the things I can,
And the wisdom to know the difference.

The Rugged Roads Of Life
Life is an ever-increasing spiral,
on the path to human perfection.
It matters not the hue of your skin,
the color of your eyes, not the color of your hair.
For self-mastery is an inner process,
that happens each time you overcome an obstacle.

43

MONEY

No one can ever determine,
the depth of your learning experience.
So continue on your journey, to overcome
your stiffest challenges,
For no one will ever know,
the depths of your overcoming.
Continue to strive for excellence in every thing you do.
For the path to fulfillment and happiness
is the rugged road of life.
−IDA GREENE

Do You Really Want Financial Success?

We create our world through our thoughts about life in general and ourselves in particular. If you are clear in your thinking and affirmative in your mind, you will find self fulfillment because you will attract positive conditions, and positive constructive people, like yourself. Though we are not able to control the circumstances of our life; we are able to control our response to people, situations, circumstances and events through our beliefs. Anything you believe in an air of positive expectancy will happen. Therefore, if you desire success, wealth, abundance, and riches believe you will achieve it. Believe this with deep feeling, and you will experience it.

To have money or be successful in dealing with money, you must first create a money mind belief or mind set. Everything is created first from a thought pattern. All ideas, plans, purpose or desires are created in your thoughts first before they become a reality. Through the natural law of correspondence, we can change any undesirable conditions. It requires the ability to control your thoughts to correspond to the desired conditions and objectives you have set in your mind. The mind can only hold one thought at a time, lack or prosperity, scarcity or abundance, poverty or wealth, success or failure. You can choose to focus on prosperity, abundance, wealth, or success.

The best way to rid yourself of a negative belief about your self, money, success or your capability is to substitute the thought for a new thought. We can never dismiss a thought. A negative thought about money, lack, or limitation can be replaced with thoughts of abundance, and prosperity. To receive more good in your life, you must open your mind to accept a greater good. For you to receive more money, you must prepare your mind to expect more wealth, abundance, and prosperity.

The following is a mental treatment by Reverend Sheila Alberts of San Diego, CA, to prepare your mind to accept a greater good. Write your name in the blank space.

This treatment is for.............................(your name)

God is love. There is only one love, and you are aware of it. You are aware that you are wanted, needed, and loved. You belong to the universe. God has not rejected you, and no one else can. You do not reject yourself. There is no condemnation or judge - ment operating through you. Every plant that my heavenly father hath not planted is rooted up and cast out. This word establishes perfect circulation, assimilation, and elimination. Whatever there is that does not belong to you is eliminated. ...., you have a consciousness of belonging to life, of feeling the divine presence, and you now accept your good! You have a complete sense of being unbur - dened, and you enter into the joy of living, which is reflected in every aspect of your experience. You have faith in yourself! The perfect action of God cast out all unlike God, and I .... give thanks that it is doing this right now for you ....

—Reverend Sheila Alberts

We must be willing to take risks, to walk forth on our faith of a perfect outcome, even though our success may not be visible.

Risk
To laugh is to risk appearing a fool.

To weep is to risk appearing sentimental.
To reach out for another is to risk involvement.
To expose feelings is to risk exposing your true self.
To place your ideas, dreams, before a crowd is
*   to risk their loss.*
To love is to risk not being loved in return.
To live is to risk dying. To hope is to risk despair.
To try is to risk failure.
But risks must be taken, because the greatest hazard in life
*   is to risk nothing.*
The person who risks nothing, does nothing, has nothing,
*   and is nothing.*
They may avoid suffering and sorrow but they cannot learn,
*   feel, change, grow, love, live.*
Chained by their certitudes, they are a slave, they have
*   forfeited their freedom. Only a person who risks is free.*
                                        —ANON

Abundance

I identify myself with abundance.
The abundance of God fills my every good desire,
*   right now.*
I surrender all fear and doubt.
I let go of all uncertainty.
The Freedom of God is my freedom.
The Power of God is my power.
I know there is no confusion, no lack of confidence.
The Presence of God is with me.
The Mind of God is my mind.
                    —GASTON GONZALEZ, GLENDALE CA

How To Get What You Want In Life

You can have anything you want
If you want it badly enough.
You can be anything you want to be,
Have, anything you set out to accomplish

If you will hold to that desire
With singleness of purpose.
                    −ROBERT COLLIER

Choose to look at your assets instead of your liabilities. Say to yourself, A nothing can interfere with the perfect right action of God The Almighty within me. I refuse to be governed by the past. Circumstances have no power over me. I now open the way for right action to express in and through my life now. I am one with my prosperity. Modified and excerpted from All About Prosperity, Jack & Cornelia Addington, DeVorss & Co. What are your assets? Write about them below.

How To Cope With The Loneliness and Isolation Of Success
The way we think and feel about ourselves is critical to how much energy, aliveness, and joy we experience daily. If our mental state is preoccupied with worry, doubt, anger, hate, or negative, warped thinking, we are likely to experience both physical and mental fatigue. When we hate ourselves, disrespect ourselves, hold ourselves in contempt, have low self-worth, or low self-esteem, it affects our total being. To be successful in anything, daily you need energy, aliveness, enthusiasm, and joy.

Are you ready for success? If you were asked this question by an unsuspecting person more than likely your immediate reply would be a resounding "yes." Then the words," why do you ask?" would probably flash across your mind or flow from your lips. Seldom, if ever will anyone ask you this question in your lifetime. Most of us are never questioned as to whether, we are ready for success by anyone, including ourselves. It is little wonder that we lack motivation and drive for our goals. How can we ever call forth our inner resources to act if we have never asked the question of ourselves? There are many questions you will need to ask of yourself before you embark on your journey of success.
The first question to ask yourself is:

   1.   Do you want success? Remember success will means

different things to different people.

2. Write your definition of business success.

The answers you have just written will help you decide if you are ready for success.

3. Ask yourself if you have the skills to handle the task/project before you?

4. Do you need to acquire further training or education? Do you have a written plan of what you will do or how long it will take to get the skills required for your profession? *Write a mini business plan now.*

   A. **Write your Mission statement now** — Your mission statement should be one that can be understood by a twelve-year-old child and recited by you without a moment's hesitation.

   B. **Write out the goal and objectives** for your business:

   C. **Write how you plan to achieve your objectives:**

   D. **Write out your Marketing Plan and Strategy:**

5. What resources (material/finances) will you need to accomplish your goal/s.

6. What plans do you have to generate the support you need be it tactical or monetary.

7. Next ask yourself, "do I have the discipline to stay focused on my dream/project. List obstacles you might face and how you will handle them.

8. Now the dual question, is this something you really want to do? Are you passionate about achieving this goal? On a scale 1-10, give yourself a number, do this every month.

9. Do you get excited each time you think about this project?

It takes courage to live in the face of adversity, when all around you is in total chaos and your world seems to be falling apart. Discouragement is a luxury you cannot afford. You need to have enough faith to believe in God's promise to you "that HE will never leave you alone nor abandon you." This brings to mind a poem by James Dillet Freeman entitled, "I am There."

I Am There
Do you need me? I am there.
You cannot see Me, yet I am the light you see by.
You cannot hear Me, yet I speak through your voice.
You cannot feel Me, yet I am the power at work in
*   your hands.*
I am at work, though you do not understand My ways.
I am at work, though you do not recognize My works.
I am not strange visions. I am not mysteries.
Only in absolute stillness, beyond self, can you know

Me as I am, and then but as a feeling and a faith.
Yet I am there. Yet I hear. Yet I answer.
When you need Me, I am there.
Even if you deny Me, I am there.
Even when you feel most alone, I am there.
Even in your fears, I am there.
Even in your pain, I am there.
I am there when you pray and when you do not pray.
I am in you and you are in Me.
Only in your mind can you feel separate from Me, for only
    in your mind are the mists of "yours" and "mine."
Yet only with your mind can you know Me and
    experience Me.
Empty your heart of empty fears.
When you get yourself out of the way I am there.
You can of yourself do nothing, but I can do all.
And I am in all.
Though you may not see the good, good is there,
    for I am there.
I am there because I have to be, because I am.
Only in Me does the world have meaning; only
    out of Me does the world go forward.
I am the law on which the movement of the stars and the
    growth of living cells are founded.
I am the love that is the law's fulfilling.
I am assurance.
I am peace. I am oneness.
I am the law that you can live by.
I am the love that you can cling to.
I am your assurance. I am your peace.
I am one with you. I Am.
Though you fail to find Me, I do not fail you.
Though your faith in Me is unsure, My faith in you never
    wavers, because I know you, because I love you.
Beloved, I am there.

—James Dillet Freeman

To Discover Your Inner Self, Ask Yourself These Questions

1. Who Am I? I am an Entrepreneur.....

2. Finish this sentence: "I am a product of my upbringing because... :

3. What I Want From Life Is:

4. My Likes Are:

    • My Dislikes Are:

5. I Am Good At Doing:

Finish this statement, "If I could only do one kind of work in life, it would be...

Daily Guide to Happiness

PRAY: *It is the greatest power on earth.*
READ: *It is the fountain of wisdom.*
GIVE: *It is too short a day to be stingy.*
PLAY: *It is the secret of perpetual youth.*
SAVE: *It is the secret of security.*
WORK: *It is the price of success.*
LOVE: *It is the road to happiness.*
CARE: *It is a God given privilege.*
LAUGH: *It is the music of the soul.*
THINK: *It is the source of power.*
                    –NORMAN VINCENT PEALE

Purpose, A Reason For Living

Purpose gives meaning to life. Purpose gives Joy, and
*   Zest to living.*
What is your Desire, your Dream?
When our eye is on our goal, we are not so easily
*   disturbed by things around us.*
Purpose awakens new trains of thoughts in our mind. Our
*   purpose directs these trains of thought into new*
*   fields of achievement.*
To succeed in life we must have some great purpose in
*   mind; some goal toward which we would like to*
*   achieve.*
Find a purpose, today!
                                        —ANON

To Discover Your Purpose In Life

1. Finish this statement, "I am the happiest when I…"

2. Finish this statement, "I am most unhappy…"

    A. When I am …

    B. When I have to …

    C. When I need to …

3. Finish this statement, "I am the happiest at work
    when I…"

4. Finish this statement, "I am most unhappy at work…"
    A. When I am …

    B. When I have to …

C. When I need to ...

5. My goals in the following areas are:

Personal

A. One year goal —

B. Five year goal —

Professional

A. One year goal —

B. Five year goal —

Spiritual

A. One year goal —

B. Five year goal —

Social

A. One year goal —

B. Five year goal —

What beliefs do you hold, that block your personal, professional, social, spiritual growth?

6. My Life's Purpose Goals are... (State a goal for the following areas and indicate a **month and year** when you plan to achieve each.)

Career Goals —

MONEY

Financial/Money Goals —

Relationship Goals —

Social Activity Goals —

To Discover Your Passion, Ask Yourself These Questions:

1. What things in life give me the greatest pleasure and satisfaction? Write these down now. Select one area where you feel least fulfilled, write about this:

   Personal:

   Professional:

   Social:

   Spiritual:

2. What things do others praise or compliment you on? Do you agree with them? Are you currently doing this type of work? If your answer is "no", Why?

   • List three ways you can develop your skills in these areas.

To Discover Your Strengths

1.   List characteristics or traits you have that set you apart from others.

2.   To find your weaknesses:
     List areas of your personality that you would like to improve.

3.   To enhance your self-image,

     A.   Ask yourself, "How do I see my self in relation to persons with similar skills?"

     B.   Create an image of what you would like to do, or become. Spend five minutes each day reflecting on the new person you will become.

Prayer Treatment For Right Employment

There is a place for me in the job market and I expect to find it. It is the right place, the position for which I am both qualified and ready. Within me as I speak is an intelligence that knows what is my right job / employment, where it is, and when I will find it. I now call upon this power to guide me in the right direction.

I release all anxiety. I await with confidence as I listen to the divine intuition which will show me the next step to take. I accept my right employment now. I am open minded and willing to be guided.

    –CHRIST CHURCH UNITY PRAYER TOWER, SAN DIEGO, CA

Chapter 5

Develop Your Self-Esteem
To Have More Money

Self Esteem, Are You Ready To Change?

Our self-esteem is a state of being, doing, acting, that allows us to appreciate ourselves, and others as valuable, and worthwhile. The person has a positive attitude, and an I am worthy, capable, competent and I can do it belief about themselves and their life. You love yourself, accept you are worthy to exist, have dreams, and have your dreams fulfilled.

There are many kinds of self-esteem, or beliefs you hold about yourself. Sometimes they do not carry over or intertwine in all areas of your life. For example your self-esteem in tennis, will not help you pass an algebra test if you have not studied algebra.

To achieve success in your chosen field, you will need to improve your self-image, and self-esteem, to believe you can become a new person with a new profession. Then, practice with your new image, and self-esteem until you are comfortable with the new you?. The areas of your self-esteem that will challenge you the most, where you will need to work diligently, and be persistent, are with your beliefs, attitudes, and acceptance of the new image, and new person you desire to become.

Your self-esteem is the medium through which you express yourself, to share the divine essence of who you are to the world. When you express from your divine essence it may or may not generate money. However, if what you do is done through a love for mankind, and a desire for God to manifest through you, the universe will compensate you generously. There are many kinds of success, and you can be successful in anything. However if love for others is not a component, it will be a hollow and empty success.

You can do many things to make money, that will lower your self-esteem, rather than elevate it, so you and others feel good about you. For example you can sell cocaine and be a success financially. However, this often involves deceit, contempt for one fellow man, greed, fears of going to jail, and doing something that violates the rights of society (you do not have the right to use your influence to bring harm to another). Also, anything you do, that you are not proud to share with the world, will negatively affect your self-esteem. This is why many of us have a crippling, self-esteem, that helps us make money but causes us to dislike ourselves, because we are "out of integrity" with ourselves, our fellow man, and life. It is easy to become comfortable with low self-esteem, because we fear change. Often what accompanies change are confusion, anger, blame, and fear of the unknown.

We are such creatures of habit, that we long for the familiar. We seek comfort and ease, rather than discomfort, and distress. Are you ready to change your beliefs, and attitude about whom you will become, to improve your self-esteem? Are you, your family, friends, and significant relationships able to accept a new you? Assess your personal skills to see where you need to improve, or change, to maximize your self-esteem success potential. Are you ready to be acknowledged, magnificent, honored, respected and appreciated? You will need to do this for yourself first, so that others can notice you and the contribution you are making to society or have made. You must learn to love yourself and have humility at the same time. It is a delicate balance, but once you achieve it, you will be a powerful magnet to attract loving relationships, money and support in your life.

Assessing Your Personal Strengths

Work, Job, or Position: **Circle One**
1. I have at least three years work experience.   Yes No
2. I have held a responsible position.   Yes No
3. I enjoy and take pride in my work.   Yes No
4. I get along with my co-workers.   Yes No
5. I feel loyal to my employer or organization. Yes No

Organizational Strengths
1. I am able to develop/short-long range goals   Yes No
2. I am able to carry out instructions.   Yes No
3. I am able to give instructions to others.   Yes No
4. I have experience organizing
    projects/events.   Yes No
5. I am goal oriented, have a sense of
    direction and purpose in my work and life.   Yes No

Relationship Strength
1. I easily meet people and am comfortable
    with them   Yes No
2. I am polite; I treat people with respect
    and consideration.   Yes No
3. I am aware of the needs and feelings
    of others.   Yes No
4. I am able listen intently to what others say. Yes No
5. I help others be aware of their strengths   Yes No

Special Aptitudes or Resources
1. I have hunches that frequently turn out
    right, and I follow through on them.   Yes No
2. I am good at my job.   Yes No
3. I am skilled in mathematics   Yes No
4. I have good public relations skills   Yes No
5. I am self motivated.   Yes No

MONEY

Developing Intellectual Strength
1. I use my reasoning ability to problem solving.   Yes No
2. I am curious intellectually.   Yes No
3. I am able to express my ideas, verbally and in writing.   Yes No
4. I am open to new ideas.   Yes No
5. I enjoy learning new things.   Yes No

Emotional Strengths
1. I am able to give, receive, affection and love.   Yes No
2. I can feel and express a wide range of emotions.   Yes No
3. I can do, or express things without hesitation.   Yes No
4. I have empathy/understand others' feelings.   Yes No
5. I understand the role of my feelings and emotions at work and at home.   Yes No

My Other Strengths
1. I have a good sense of humor and I am able to laugh at myself   Yes No
2. I like to try new things, and new horizons.   Yes No
3. I am able to take a risk, grow, and develop my potential.   Yes No
4. I have perseverance and stick-to-itiveness.   Yes No
5. I take care of my health and look my best.   Yes No

PERSONAL STRENGTHS ASSESSMENT

Tally your score. Give yourself one point for each yes. There is no optimum number of yes or no answers. Use this as a tool to notice areas where you are strong or need to improve.

To have a healthy self-esteem you must be: flexible, open to change, able to laugh at your mistakes, creative, continue seeking ways to grow and improve, ask question when you do not understand, give yourself freedom to say no, and yes, take time to pause-catch your breath, and start again.

Listen to your body — understand when it says, take time to smell the roses, meditate, smile, cry, laugh, give thanks to God for blessings received. Remember the highest form of prayer is gratitude.

We wear our attitude outside us. It is written on our faces, and broadcast through our body language. What messages are you sending to others about your self-esteem, positive or negative?

- What is the status of your self-esteem/self-image, self-appreciation or self-depreciation?

- How do you feel about yourself, do you like yourself?

- What is your belief about your ability to get or have money?

- Do you see yourself having money?How much money?

Is this image comfortable or uncomfortable for you?

Self Esteem Assessment

1. Who am I? (Be specific, avoid global remarks.)

2. Do I have a negative image of myself,

3. What makes you special/unique? Be specific, list five or moretraits/characteristics.

4. Do you value your unique gifts and talents? List attributes or talents you possess.

5. Does your self-worth comes from inside or outside you? Do you look to others to define who you are or what you are capable of doing?

6. Do you see yourself as a struggler, who just has enough resources and money to "get by" or do you see yourself as possessing the necessary potential to achieve what you desire in life?

7. What are some ways you can acknowledge yourself without ridiculing others who are different ?

8. In what ways can you communicate positively and openly with others if you are shy or reserved? :

9. List some things you can do to make friends with strangers or become a better conversationalist:

10. How can you let those of the opposite sex know you want to be their friend, or converse with them as an acquaintance?

11. Some things you can do to overcome shame or embarrassment of yourself and/or your family:

12. Since our self-image is an outward projection of our dreams and desires; what plans do you have to readjust the way you see yourself, so it is aligned with your new self-image/self-esteem? :

13. My old beliefs about me were:

14. My new beliefs about me are:

15. My old attitude about me was:

16. My new attitude about me is:

17. Self-Acceptance is not blinding yourself to your faults, nor hating yourself for them, but claiming, and accepting you can change for the better. And holding to your vision of the new you, even though it may not be apparent to you or anyone. Write what you will do to create a new you below.

> A. My old self-acceptance was:

> B. My new self-acceptance is:

18. My old Money Self-Image was:

19. My new Money Self-Image is:

DESIDERATA

Go placidly amid the noise and the haste and remember what peace there may be in silence. As far as possible without surrender, be on good terms with all people. Speak your truth quietly and clearly; and listen to others, even to the dull and ignorant; they too have their story. Avoid loud and aggressive persons; they are vexatious to the spirit. If you compare yourself with others, you may become vain or bitter, for always there will be greater or lesser persons than yourself.

Enjoy your achievements as well as your plans. Keep interested in your own career, however humble; it is a real possession in the changing fortunes of time. Exercise caution in your business affairs, for the world is full of trickery. But let this not blind you to what virtue there is ; many persons strive for high ideals, and everywhere life is full of heroism. Be yourself. Especially do not feign affection. Neither be cynical about love; for in the face of all aridity and disenchantment, it is as perennial as the grass.

Take kindly the counsel of the years, gracefully surrendering the things of youth. Nurture strength of spirit to shield you in sudden misfortune. But do not distress yourself with dark imaginings. Many fears are borne of fatigue and loneliness. Beyond a wholesome discipline, be gentle with yourself. You are a child of the Universe no less than the trees and the stars; you have a right to be here. And whether or not it is clear to you, no doubt the universe is unfolding as it should.

Therefore, be at peace with God, whatever you conceive him to be, and whatever your labors and aspirations in the noisy confusion of life, keep peace in your soul. With all its sham drudgery, and broken dreams, it is still a beautiful world.

Be cheerful. Strive to be happy.

Affirm for yourself

I acknowledge the divine , glorious, magnificent person that I am. Since I am made in the image, and likeness of God, I allow this unlimited power to guide and direct my life. I give up all sense of smallness to express my divine unlimited potential.

Affirm for yourself

Today I accept all my gifts and talents. I am amazed how blessed I am.

DOLLY SEWELL, NOTTINGHAM, ENGLAND

Through Our Desires And Goals We Become Motivated To Change Our Life

1. My 1-year, 5-, and 10-year goals in the following areas are: (Write **month** and **year** you will achieve **each goal**)

   Personal/Family —

   Education/Study —

   Social/Friendship —

   Spiritual/Religious —

Start now and enjoy the rest of your life. "*Life Is Shorter Than You Think.*"

To Discover Your Career Niche, Ask Yourself These Questions:

1. What things in life give you the greatest pleasure or satisfaction? Write these down then put them in order of #1 greatest satisfaction, #2, etc.
   1.
   2.
   3.
   4.
   5.
   Personal:

Future Career Goals:

Social Goals:

Spiritual Goals:

2. What things do others praise or compliment you on?
    List below.

3. Now that you have completed the activities above,
    what thing or things would you enjoy doing every day
    of the year, even if you were not paid monetarily?
    Whatever you choose is your "hot button."

I Am Worth It

I may sometime cause confusion when I am unclear in my
*   communication, unsure of myself, or uncertain about*
*   an outcome, yet I am worth the bother.*
I may act timid and fearful sometimes, but please remem -
*   ber that I am trying to sort things out in my mind, and*
*   I am worth the bother.*
Even though you may struggle to understand me,
*   I am worth it.*
My friend, I am the other half of you.
I am incomplete without you, and you are incomplete
*   without me.*
In some strange way, though we differ in racial
*   composition, thoughts,*

ideas, and behavior; we are wedded to each other.
I will release you for now, to soar above the heavens.
Just remember that whatever disappointment or
challenge I face,
I deserve the best, for I am worth it.
IDA GREENE

Quotes by the Masters

An optimist is a person who sees the green light everywhere,
while a pessimist sees only the red stoplight...
The truly wise person is color-blind.
–ALBERT SCHWEITZER

We could all save ourselves a lot of words if we'd only remem -
ber that people really take advice when they have to pay for it.
–WILLIAM BLAKE

You have only to work up imagination to the state of vision,
and the thing is done.
–WILLIAM BLAKE

The Law of Faith is founded upon the recognition that we
know more than we have read, heard, or studied; we know
more because we are more; we have a direct link to univer -
sal wisdom; we only have to look, listen, and trust.
–DAN MILLMAN

Chapter 6

How To Become
A Magnet For Money

Mentally see yourself as abundant, see abundance all around you. In your mind see an abundance of water, air, grass, trees and on these leaves see green leaves, then see dollar signs on these leaves.

Money and success is created from your self expression. And your self-expression is a spiritual quality. You are here in life to express your God potential. Do not confuse your Divine self expression with your livelihood. When you allow God to express through you, all your needs will be met. Never accept a job, or engage in any activity just for money. Because if you do not express your divine essence, and God given talents, you will become unhappy, bored, and lose enthusiasm for life and living. When you lose your enthusiasm, you lose your light. Jesus said, " Ye are the light of the world." You must be alive, joyous, and aglow. When you do work you enjoy, it fulfills a divine purpose in the universe, and everyone benefits from it.

Money is not evil, it does serve a purpose. We need it to secure goods and services to make life comfortable for ourselves. You can also assist those less fortunate than yourself. Just remember to circulate money, never hoard it, use it rightly, treat it with respect and you will always have it. Money is good. Everything that God created is good. Money is like love, you can circulate it, use, but you can not own, or possess it. Money is a spiritual entity and so are you. Money is a great tool to help you refine your inner essence and divine nature. If you use it rightly you will always have it. It is like the wind and the ocean, it comes and it goes. Just as the ocean has its ebb and tide so does money. You breathe in and you breathe out. The breathe always return. You can never be without air, the ocean or money. You can get and keep money by allowing it to circulate. Let it flow in and out of your life and you will keep it.

You are a spiritual being, in a human body, having a spiritual experience. Your primary purpose to be on the planet, is to use your divine self expression to grow spiritually, and become a Master like Jesus. We must first master our physical body, before we can achieve mastery in our spiritual life. We do this through right thinking, right living, and right divine self-expression. Success is not just about desire, power, and money. It is a spiritual and sacred journey. Life is the journey into your soul, where you express your true essence of joy, truth, beauty, prosperity, peace, abundance, harmony, tranquility, contentment, fulfillment, love and eternal bliss

Both life and success are about your journey, learned experiences, and personal growth. We grow through each challenge we encounter. No challenge you experience in life will leave you where it found you. Each experience teaches us how to be more humble, gentle, loving, compassionate, and how to forgive without taking things personally. You are here in this life to become your Divine-Self. We become our Christ-Self by listening and responding to the intuition God give us, which is designed to bring forth the best aspects of our nature: Gentleness, Compassion, Loving, Understanding, Tender, Helpful, Supportive, Ethical, Friendly, and Peaceful, bring out the best in ourselves and others. Never worship money. Worship the Goddess or God inside you. It is your true source of power.

We came from God, and to God we return when we complete our earths' journey. Remember, what you are is Gods' gift to you, and what you make of yourself is your gift to God. Will you return to God the same raw materials given you on your entrance to planet earth; or will you return to God a grand masterpiece. A work of art so magnificent to behold, that all the celestial angels and hosts take a bow. They bow because you fought a good fight. You put your best effort into everything you did. You used your work, creativity, talents, relationships, friendships, and painful life experiences to reach a higher level of service to your fellow man.

We were created to serve and be of service to our fellow man and woman. We serve God when we serve our fellow man. When we can let go our pride, prejudice, possessions, our envy, jealousy, hurt feelings, our anger, and our ego; we take on angelic qualities and become healer of the planet.

You were given dreams, goals, and aspirations to refine your temperament, your spirit, attitude, and to become more loving. Whenever you accomplish any goal, you set out to do, and achieve it in spite of hardship, or challenge you are a success. .

Financial success for you, may not be the same for another person. God speaks to each of us individually. We are each marching to a different drummer.

The amount of money you have or will acquire will depend upon your thoughts. Money or financial success is an inside job. You must first create it within your mind, before it will out picture in the real world of manifestation. And to create it in your mind you must do two things: You must be willing to do whatever is necessary to heal your mind of the belief that you are separate from God and his good and change your thoughts or word associations in relation to money. Do this exercise now

Money Association Test

Fear	Confusion	Indecision	Conflict
Guilt	Excitement	Tension	Confidence
Anxiety	Superiority	Respect	Problems
Inferiority	Worry	Envy	Love
Friends	Aggression	Hate	Happiness
Evil	Considerate	Helpful	Kind

1. Write four word associations with money
    A.
    B.
    C.
    D.

2. Write about how these word associations influence your relationship with money either positively or negatively.

3. What did you learn about you and your relationship with money?

Our goal is see ourselves as one with God and his good. We are All were created by the One God. There is one energy source, one life force, and one Divine Spirit that unites all people as one. We can tap into this energy source to create health, wealth, or anything that is pure, noble, loving, harmonious, and serves all of humanity.

God is the source of all prosperity and abundance. To acquire wealth, or be successful, you must be a larger channel for God to pour through into the universe. Your goal, is to discover what is your talent, and to find a way to give your gift to the world. Reverend Margaret Wright feels *The key to prosperity and abundance is to give.* **"The more you give, the more you get,"** Give of your time, talent, and treasure." and be more of a person that someone would want to be with in a business relationship. I agree with her philosophy. Whenever, I am short of money, I find someone to whom I can give money. It helps me to prime the pump and get my money circulating, so it can circulate back to me

Never compare your success or achievements with any other person. Only God is the judge, not you or another. For just when you think you have failed, God says, well done my good and faithful servant, you have fought a good fight. You are a success.

.Never lose your faith or hope. My mother used to always say where there is a will, there is a way. Believe that God will show you the way to get and have what you need in life. Sometimes, we are tested so that we can develop courage, tenacity, faith, love, compassion, gentleness, and patience. My life's lesson has been and continues to be, for me to develop a more compassionate heart. Learn to be patient, to Let Go and Let God, meaning to Trust God or Have Faith that God will provide for all my needs including money.

The tool you will need to achieve success in anything will be a positive self-image anchored in faith. Faith is a positive, mental state of knowing, that even though the outcome may be bleak, look hopeless, and impossible, that the perfect outcome you desire will manifest. Faith is the space where you let go, and grab onto the unknown, God. With faith you have to believe, and know, before it is manifested. Faith is letting Go and letting God take over. The human mind wants to know the outcome before it happens, because we like to be in control of things. If control is your issue, you will have little faith, abundance, prosperity, wealth, or success. Faith is about being out of control. It is letting go your control, to discover new horizons. Faith is about gratitude. What can you be thankful for today. The following exercise can help you develop a more positive attitude, the foundation for financial success and the accumulation of money.

I feel good when I think of money.
> **Say To Yourself:**
> *I Affirm My money will be used to good purpose. Today I start a new day, a new month, a new year and I am a new me. I accept that I am success, I am successful in all I do, or will become.*
> **I am a secure and confident person.** *I express myself as a confident and secure person. I communicate easily with everyone about how I live my life with zest, energy and enthusiasm. I am real with everyone. I am a happy*

person just as I am. I am a very energetic, powerful and enthusiastic being of love. I am committed to being a secure and confident person.

I feel spiritually connected with each person I talk to. *I communicate naturally from my heart-space at all times with all beings. I am about being powerful, all-loving and giving gentle warm wisdom to all beings on Earth. I see the Divine within everyone and I easily communicate this to them. I am confident and comfort - able looking directly into any human beings eyes. I can now approach any person I meet with a genuine smile, open heart and a positive mental attitude. I am protect - ed at all times because I am an infinite loving source to all people. I am committed to feeling spiritually con - nected with each person to whom I talk.*

My body and mind are radiating with perfect fitness and health. *I am experiencing a higher level of physi - cal, mental, emotional strength, spiritual strength and vitality every day. I am committed to work out and I eas - ily do each exercise. I am happy about my life and my body shows it. I now exercise in a healthy, loving and meditative way. I am committed to living in a mind and body that are radiating with perfect fitness and health.*

I speak from my heart in challenging situations. *I awake each morning trusting that it is safe to be in my heart all day long. I can live my from my heart and it is safe to love from my heart. My heart is continuously expanding & deepening with feelings of peace and love. I now feel a divine love radiating from my whole body, out to everyone on earth. I am committed to speak from my heart during challenging situations.*

I sleep deeply and rest completely every night. *I awaken each morning feeling refreshed, full of energy, and enthusiasm for the day.*

Excellence Has No Fear of Observation

Therefore when you are being your best, it does not matter if other person watches you.

The 4 Way Test of the Rightness of What You Think, Say or Do, ask yourself:

1. Is it the TRUTH?
2. Is it FAIR to all Concerned?
3. Will it Build GOODWILL and Better Friendships?
4. Will it Be BENEFICIAL to All Concerned?

If your answer is yes to all the above, you will be a huge success in your chosen endeavor and in life.

Responsibility

1. *Responsibility means accepting the importance of the job we do. Work that we value is the only work that is valuable.*

2. *Responsibility means seeing things from a point-of-view big enough to include the people and the organi - zation around us.*

3. *Responsibility means taking criticism as it is intended: an attempt to improve the quality of our efforts, with - out ridiculing us as people.*

4. *Responsibility means accepting the little, essential dis - ciplines that go with any team operation — punctuali - ty, neatness safety.*

5. *Responsibility means realizing that the situation at work is like the situation at home — every single thing we do affects someone else, for better or worse.*

6. *Responsibility means accepting problems and difficul - ties as a normal part of any job. If we had no prob - lems, we would win no victories, and without victories, life would be pretty drab.*

7. *Responsibility means looking at your complaints to see if they have solutions, or if you're just complaining about things that can't possibly be changed. Complain*

to someone who can do something to effect the change you want; back room complaints only make everyone unhappy. Be constructive — identify what you see as needing change, and then give positive suggestions about how you think changes can be made.

—ANON

Positive Self-Regard Affirmations

I behave as an equal to all persons.

I am smart.

I am intelligent.

I am knowledgeable.

I am competent.

I accept my goodness.

I am perfect, just as I am.

Affirm

Today there is nothing I can do, say, think, or become that estab - lishes my worth, my self-worth comes from God.

THINGS I WILL CHANGE AS OF TODAY

I Now Affirm:

I like me! I like the person I am becoming.

I trust my judgment, and my decision making ability.

That my mind is as good as that of another person.

My mind will work for me and I can make wise decisions.

That I have an excellent memory.

That I can depend on my mind to remember things.

That I can figure things out with my keen, sharp, mind.

That I can release all anger, resentment, and unhappy thoughts from the past to be free.

It is O.K. for me to make a mistake.

It is O.K. for me to not be perfect.

It is O.K. for me to not know everything.

It is O.K. for me to be criticized.

It is O.K. for me to relax, and be me.

It is O.K. for me to enjoy life.

Winners vs. Losers

The winner is always a part of the answer;

The Loser is always a part of the problem;

The Winner always has a program;

The Loser always has an excuse;

The Winner says "Let me do It for you;"

The Loser says, "That's not my job;"

The Winner sees an answer for every problem;

The Loser sees a problem for every answer;

The Winner sees a green near every sand trap;

The Loser sees two sand traps near every green;

The Winner says, "It may be difficult but it's possible."

The Loser says, "It may be possible, but it's too difficult."

Chapter 7

How To Get And Keep
The Money All The Time

How to Have Mastery Over Money

You will fail for one of three reasons in your effort to master money: 1. Lack of clarity; 2. Lack of congruency; 3. Lack of consistency.

Money is cyclical, it comes and it goes. Do not worry when it is not visible. Just be open to follow the essence of your heart. God will lead you to where your essence matches on the highest levels. You sell your house, because your essence no longer matches its essence and change jobs for the same reason. It is the same with money. When you believe this, you will never have a problem with money, things, or places. God wants to give you great abundance. Thinking lack depletes your soul. People who live in poverty work very hard; poverty is hard work. It does not matter what is the poverty-poverty of mind, poverty of body, poverty of spirit-all are the same.

When you understand how you think about money or things, the energy will shift and all your worry about money will disappear once and for all. You must be aware of your thought processes, and how it manifests continuously. Ask for Divine guidance to see your inner Truth and how your essence connects with the idea of money. It is not your mothers' or sisters' thoughts about money, it is what you think and feel about money that matters. When you no longer experience anxiety or fear about your lack of money, and have confidence it will be available when you need it; you will be at peace with money. Then money or its equivalent will never be a problem for you again.

Pray and ask your guardian angels to help you to be clear about money and how you relate to it.

MONEY

Money, How To Get And Keep It

You can work for someone or go into business for yourself as a means to generate money. Whichever you choose, there are five areas you will want to address, when putting together a business plan for yourself or seeking your ideal career path. The five areas you will want to address are: Write something next to the words below.

Keywords —
Key sentences —
Key paragraph —
Key content —
Key credibility —

The six-part process to define your ideal job or career is to:
Position yourself by concept
1. What do you do?
2. How well do you do it?
3. Why should someone hire you?
4. What are you really all about?
5. Ask the courage questions.
   a. Does this make sense?
   b. Would you like to work with me?
   c. Is this the type of program you are looking for?
6. Ask how can we work together?

Have a meaningful conversation with the other person. Learn to end your conversation with your four main areas of focus and ask the courage type questions.

Get outside your normal environment and refocus your efforts in growing your business and reaching the level of success you desire. Here are key words, to use as a guide in your business:
1. **Direction** — Make sure you are heading in the right direction
2. **Identity** — Create or recreate a proper identity that serves you from a visual and verbal perspective
3. **Marketing** — Create a game-plan that gets you visible, busy and booked with the right business.

4. **Benchmarks** — when focused and on track, how to set up a system for accountability, and self-renewal

The Money Will Follow

People who try something new – perhaps they take a hobby or keen interest and turn it into a viable business, or they change careers and move from one field to another – have to be good at "letting go." They must be capable of sensing when it is the right time to move and when it is best to wait. Some people are naturally intuitive about their risk-taking. Others use risks as a way of doing themselves in: their self-defeating scripts, their low self-evaluation and their lack of experience can create poor judgment calls about "letting go." Almost everyone, good risk-taker and not so good, wants a formula to help him take risks. Unfortunately what works for one may not work for another. Nothing can take us off the book of being individually responsible for our life decisions.

Next, there is a "waiting period" … what we do while we wait is also a matter of judgment, choice an faith. IT is during this waiting period that we must, individually, learn to "read" the situation. This is when many people, after a period of evaluation, decide that they do not have the talent or temperament to continue. Perhaps they, like a client of mien who started her own business, realize that they prefer the excitement of working with a large company instead of the solitary, lonely atmosphere of being the chief cook and bottle washer, the head, hands, and tail of the organization.

The third aspect of "the money will follow" is the ability to think well of ourselves and our capabilities, even without money. It is important to acknowledge that each person who embarks upon a new vocational path may be subject to strong negative self-opinions if money is not forthcoming quickly or in ample supply. This is certainly true in America where we typically equate success and money. The successful person, in our society, is the one who has a great deal of money. The unsuccessful person is the one who is poor. Our own self-evaluation – our subjective comfort and discomfort – is critical during the early stages of waiting for financial security because it can trigger unproductive actions during this person.

Excerpt from Do What You Love, The Money Will Follow *by Marsha Sinetar, Dell Publishing.*

The ABCs of Money Prayer Treatment

Purpose: I accept my wealth and its growth.

You do not need to be poor like your parents.

Say to yourself, *It is okay for me to have wealth.*

Recite the following prayer treatment:

Recognition: *Oh beautiful Infinite, Radiant God, I acknowledge that abundance, growth and expansion are the natural laws of the Universe.*

Unification: *The sufficiency of the Universe is mirrored in my world. I know that my life expands, encompassing more Godness, more goodness, more ownership of my wholeness, more joy, and more wealth.*

Realization: *I am safe. I am whole. I accept that I am ever sup - ported by the Universe. Just as there is enough air for me and for all others to breathe, there is enough time, enough money, enough talent for me and all others. It is safe to trust. My trust is well placed. I openly and freely magnetize and accept wealth and riches in my life. I welcome all forms of wealth... a wealth of time, a wealth of generosity, a wealth of joy, a wealth of kind - ness, a wealth of gentleness, and a wealth of money. My accounts increase. I receive my expanded wealth. I am worthy. I accept my wealth. My actions support me. An elegant suffi - ciency is reflected everywhere. My natural state is growth and unlimited expansion.*

Acceptance: *I accept my power. I am comfortable with my rich - es. My wealth feels at home with me.*

Thanksgiving: *Thank you for revealing my true nature of abun - dance. I am filled with joy and gratitude. I dwell inside the joy and humble thankfulness as my ever present companions.*

Release: *I let this prayer go, knowing that I have but to speak it my word and it is. The Law of Attraction magnetizes me and my good. All that I seek, is seeking me. And So It Is. Amen.*

—ANON

Affirmations to Train Your Mind to Manifest Money

I Am Experiencing an Abundance of Money, NOW!

MONEY in Abundance is God in Action, in the form of Plenty, plenty to enjoy and to share.

MONEY circulated abundantly is the channel for the exchange of unlimited Good!

MONEY is Blessing me now. I am Abundant NOW!

MONEY flows freely in my experience, now Blessing my bank account with Abundance to spend and to share with others.

MONEY flows freely in my experience now Blessing my creditors with my bills paid, and opening more doors for me to use more money in my life.

MONEY flows freely in my household, now Blessing my relatives and friends with more to spend and to share with others.

MONEY flows freely in my profession, now Blessing my job and co-workers with more to spend and to share with others.

MONEY flows freely in my Church, now Blessing the Ministry of my Church and Its Congregation with more to spend and to share with others.

MONEY flows freely in my country, now Blessing our government, our people, and the whole world with more money to spend and to share with others.

I am receiving unexpected income now, from unexpected places, people, and institutions, as I declare my divine right to prosperity I must be blessed with plenty. And I am sharing now 10% of all unexpected money received with the sender of this prayer. Thank You God for abundance. AMEN

For Best Results: During the coming month, use this Prayer/ Treatment at least three times a day, first thing in the morning, at

noon and before bedtime. Read it aloud (if possible) and meditate upon it. God is Blessing you now with unlimited prosperity.

Say aloud to yourself:

*I give thanks that I am now rich, well and happy and
that my financial affairs are in divine order. Every day
in every way I am growing richer and richer.*

*Money, Money, Money, manifest thyself here and
now in rich abundance.*

*I am one with the Divine substance. I am the com -
plement of God. I am the Christ of God. All that, God
has and is I am. I claim my rich and Divine inheri -
tance as a child of the most high. Watch your thoughts
when you are handling your money, because your
money is attached through your mind to the one
source of substance and all money. When you think of
your money, which is visible, as something directly
attached to an invisible source that is giving or with -
holding according to your thought, you have the key to
all riches and reason for all lack.*

—CHARLES FILLMORE

Think Wealth To Create Financial Success

Your thoughts create your reality. What you think about grows
because that is where you focus your energy. Everything that
exists today was once a thought in somebody's mind. This
thought became reality through taking action in a focused way. So
in order to create success in the world, we must first develop
thought patterns that are aligned with our vision of success.

A human mind generates approximately 50,000 thoughts per
day, and many of them are the same thoughts as yesterday. How
many new thoughts do you have per day? Do you spend your
time recycling the same old thoughts, or do you continuously fill
your mind with new ideas? In order to bring about positive
change in your life, you must create new empowering thought
patterns in your brain. Old thoughts just create the same old thing,
while new thoughts can create success in any area of your life.

What thoughts are currently controlling your life? Do you

know what you spend the most time thinking about? Write about it now

Learn to believe and trust the Divine plan in the universe, it is an orderly causation, which I refer to as God. Trust God and His Creation called Money. Can you trust that a leaf exit and will continue to reproduce again and again? It is green, small and you can carry a lot of them easily. However, a leaf has no value as money because no one trusts it. You have to start somewhere, so why not trust that money will reproduce itself again and again . If one person can have money in amounts equal to or exceeding their needs, then so can you. If one can have, then so can you. If none can have, then, neither can you. If God gives money to one person, you can have it too. If he gives money to one, then it is all's. If all have it, like leaves, then it has value. It is all in the mind as is the value of anything.

It is important that you **believe** money works. When you **believe** money can be yours, it will be. When you **believe,** you will have enough money, you will. When you **believe**, you are abundantly, gifted to have anything you desire, you will have it. *When you separate yourself from this belief, you will not have money.*

The 10 Commandments for Raising Your Manifesting Vibration
1. I will replace worry with wonder.
2. I will cancel and replace thoughts like I... "should", "could", "would", "have to", "must", "need to" and "I've got to" with "I want to", "I get to", "I'd like to", "I'd love to" "I can".
3. I will accept, approve and appreciate I love my life exactly as it is, no matter what the experience life is offering me.
4. I will explore each experience in life (especially those I have trouble with) with an innocent childlike curiosity.
5. I will be independent of the good and bad opinions of others.

6. I will remain centered and at peace with myself when others are not.
7. I will only say positive empowering things to or about others in a way they can understand.
8. I will exercise, meditate, eat healthy, and get enough sleep at least 6 days a week.
9. I will open myself to others and create long term fulfilling loving relationships.
10. I will be 100% committed to these amazing life transformational commitments for the next 90 days.

Prosperity Through the Love Concept

Consistent practice of the Love Concept
Is one of the quickest ways to overcome all of your
  difficulties
And demonstrate your spiritual heritage of unlimited good.
The way to practice the Love Concept is to become filled
  with the idea of Love inwardly, and then express it
  both inwardly and outwardly.
This releases a high-powered energy that is instantly felt
  and responded to by people and situations.
Practicing the Love Concept can do more to help you
  achieve your goals
Than all the hard mental effort in the world.
If you get too tense about what you want out of life and try
  to force it into Manifestation mentally.
You can actually repel the very good you are trying
  to manifest.
Use the Love Concept
Magnetically draws your good to you in countless ways.
This method takes the strain out of demonstrating
  your good.
The universe is not responding to your language.
The universe is responding to your vibration
And your vibration is about the way you feel.
–FLORENCE SHEN The Game of Life and How to Play It

Check the Answer that Applies About Your Relationship With Money Below:

Statement	Sometimes	Always	Seldom	Never
1. I am aware of my relationship with money.				
2. I usually fold my money neatly and look at it longingly before placing it in my wallet.				
3. I have positive and loving feelings about money.				
4. I plan how I will use my money.				
5. I know where my money goes.				
6. I feel good about letting go of my money.				
7. I know without a doubt that my money is being used to bring about "good" on the				
8. I love what money represents to me.				
9. I am fearful that I will not have enough money to meet my needs.				
10. I can prioritize the things I buy into A, B, C categories. A being the things I need immediately. B the things I can postpone. C the thing I can get a month to a year later.				
11. I can discipline myself with money because I am not afraid that I will run out of my supply.				
12. I accept that money is a spiritual entity.				

MONEY

Understanding Your Relationship to Money

What is your relationship with money? Are you comfortable being around money or do you feel fearful and tense, do your hands feel sweaty, does your heart palpate fast? Can you think clearly when you are around money or do your childhood fears surface? What are some of your limiting beliefs about that money that keeps money away from you? Write some of these beliefs down now. Example: I feel money will change me from being a nice person to being self-centered, egotistical, greedy, conniving, crooked — add other words or phrases you feel apply to you.

If you inherited a large sum of money, say, one million dollars, what would be some of your fears about your ability to have or manage the money? List your fears below: Example: I fear money would change me into being....

Think of something specific you want to manifest now. Notice how your body reacts when you think about it. Does your heart open and expand, or does it tighten and contract? If you feel an expansive and opening sensation that makes your heart feel joyful, excitement, energy, and passion, you are focusing your manifesting energies in the right direction. If on the other hand, you get a sense of feeling apprehensive, afraid, bored, apathetic, or tired when you think of manifesting the thing you desire, you will most likely not achieve your desire.

It can be difficult to know what you really want since there are sometimes many voices inside of us which often want opposite things. A great way to distinguish the healthy from the not-so-healthy voices is to notice if there is a "should" involved. If there is, you will feel tired most of the time, and feel everything is a burden, and experience tension in your body, the end result will be a decrease of your manifestation abilities. When what you want comes from your heart, and is not based on the expectations or desires of someone else, you will manifest the desire easily, without effort, when you do it because you want and choose to do it. If you think you "should" manifest something because of society's expectations or what your dad, mom or family want or expects of you, you will struggle with having a lack of energy, freedom, and enjoyment. A true desire comes from your heart, your inner source of inspiration, and is uniquely yours.

Remember, in order to manifest something effortlessly, it has to be important to you and you are passionate about it. So check inside your heart and feelings on what you have a passion for. When we are passionate about anything we do it without struggle, effort, or complaint. I am passionate about counseling children, and I would do it even if I were not paid. I can be over booked, dead tired, yet I will find a way to counsel a child, even if it is for 10 minutes at 10 pm. I love speaking and I am good at it. You can awaken me at 3 am, and I am ready to speak. I have a speech in my brain that automatically comes out of my mouth. The words are always on target and I am amazed at the wisdom that flows through me. You have to be passionate about getting or having money.

Another reason why you may lack money even though you want it may be the result of fear. Often we are afraid to acquire or get money, because of a conditioned fear we inherited from our parents. We live in a fear-based society, so we have many fears. We are afraid to acquire or get money and then, if we acquire or get money, we become afraid we will lose it or some-one will take it away from us. The goal for us in relation to money is to let go and suspend all fear surrounding money. We can never be without money. We cannot have or lose something that is a part of our emotional makeup. Money comes from God; it is a part of God. God is what we originated from; we can never be without God, our source of life. Both God and money are tied to our life source. There is an inborn instinct in us to survive and thrive. You have to decide how small or big you want to live. It is alright to act small, live small and be small as long as you have a desire to grow expand, live large and have more "Good" or God in your life. You can serve a massive number of people when you think big, play big, act big and have a lot of money, or you can think small, play small, act small and have little money. The choice is yours. You can change your thinking (thoughts) and change your life.

I used to think, "I do not have a lot of money because I am too lazy to do the things to acquire and get money". Finally, I had to admit to myself that I harbored negative thoughts about money and my ability to get and have money. I started working on my self-worth, and deservedness. I had to accept that I was worthy and deserving of money. That God wanted me to have money, because he wanted me to serve his children, and I needed lots of money to complete the task. It became O.K for me to have money for my non-profit organization that served At-risk children. I had to work on my money self-image to have more, be more, and enjoy more of the "Good things of life". I decided that I was a good person, and I deserved good things to happen to me. I made a decision that money would not change me from being the loving, caring, compassionate person, I perceived myself to be and that it was a good thing for me to get and keep money.

You will have to decide if you can trust yourself to get manage and have a lot or a small amount of money. Now that you know how to get and keep money, the choice is yours whether you will do it.

GUIDE TO MONEY TERMINOLOGY

Accrued Interest	The pro-rate interest obligation that has accumulated since a bond's last payment date. Most bonds trade at a price that reflects their net market price plus accrued interest. Defaulted and certain other bonds, however, trade "flat," which means without any allowance for accrued interest.
Acid-Test Or Quick Ratio	Cash and accounts receivable divided by current liabilities; used to measure short-term liquidity.
Asset	Any item of value; often income-producing; appears on left side of balance sheet.
Balanced Fund	A mutual fund that invests in both stocks and bonds.
Balance Sheet	A financial statement providing an instant picture of a firm's or individual's financial position; lists assets, liabilities, and net worth.
Bear Market	A declining market.
Broker	An employee of a financial intermediary who acts as an agent in the buying and selling of securities. Unlike a dealer, a broker never owns the securities that he or she trades for his or her customers.
Bull Market	A rising market.
Capital Asset	Virtually any investment asset. To qualify as a capital asset, an asset must be held as an investment rather than in inventory as an item of trade.
Cash Flow	Reported profits plus depreciation, depletion, and amortization.
Cash Market	A market where physical commodities (spot) are traded for cash.

MONEY

Commodity

In general, any article of commerce; in investment terminology; any of a select group of items traded on one of the commodity exchanges. Such commodities are traded either spot (for immediate delivery) or in the futures market (for delivery at a pre-specified future date).

Common Stock

Represents proportional ownership of an incorporated enterprise. Common stockholders are the residual claimants for assets after all holders of debt and preferred stock have received their contractual payments.

Compound

Returns are compounded by reinvesting one period's income earn

Interest

Additional income the following period. Thus at 9 percent compounded annually, $100 will yield $9 the first year. In the following year the 9 percent will be applied to $109 for a return of $9.81. In the third year the principal will have grown to $118.81 $(100 + 9 + 9.81)$ and another 9 percent will add about $10.62. This process continues with the interest rate being applied to a larger and larger principal. While the above example assumes that the compounding takes place annually, the process can occur more frequently.

Current Assets

that are expected to be used up or converted to cash within the next year or next operating period, whichever is longer. Cash, accounts receivable, and inventory are the major types of current assets.

Current

Liabilities that will become due in the next year or the next

Liabilities

Operating cycle, whichever is longer.

	Current liabilities include accounts payable, short-term bank loans, the current portion of long-term debt, and taxes payable.
Debt-Equity	The ratio of total debt to total equity.
Decreasing Term	A type of term insurance in which protection decreases with the insured's age.
Depreciation	A deduction from income that allocates the cost of fixed assets over their useful lives.
Dollar Averaging	A formula-investment plan requiring periodic (such as monthly) fixed-dollar-amount investments. This practice tends to "average" the unit purchase cost of an investment made over time.
Equity or Net Estate	Assets minus liabilities. An individual's residual ownership A person's total worth as determined by his or her vested interests in property and other assets, exclusive of any liabilities.
Growth Fund	A common-stock mutual fund that seeks price appreciation by concentrating on growth stocks.
Growth Stock	The shares of a company that is expected to achieve rapid growth; such shares often carry above-average risks and price/earnings ratios.
Income Statement	A financial statement of a firm's or individual's interim earnings; shows how revenues were spent and how much remains as net income.
Incorporation	The forming of a business into a legal body endowed with various rights and duties.
Interest	The amount a borrower pays for the use of a lender's funds; is frequently expressed as an annual percentage of the principal balance

outstanding and may be compounded on a monthly, quarterly, annual, or some other periodic basis.

Investment — Any asset expected to yield deferred benefits.

IRA Individual — A retirement plan that allows employees to set aside up to $2,000 annually into a tax-sheltered instrument. Earnings on the IRA Retirement Funds are tax-protected. The contributed sum can also have tax advantages if the individual is not covered by a company pension and/or has a relatively low income.

Keogh Account — A retirement account that allows self-employed individuals to set aside up to $30,000 or 20 percent of their income into a tax-sheltered fund. Both the contributions and the earnings on it are not subject to tax until they are withdrawn.

Line of Credit — Prearranged agreement from a lender to supply up to some maximum a loan at pre-specified terms.

Long-Term — Liabilities that are not due in the next year or next operating

Liabilities — period, whichever is shorter; usually includes outstanding bonds, debentures, mortgages, term loans, etc.

Marketability — The ease with which an investment can be bought or sold, without appreciably affecting its price. For example, blue-chip stocks are usually highly marketable, since they are actively traded.

Money Fund — A mutual fund that invests in short-term highly-liquid securities.

Money Market	The market for high-quality, short-term securities, such as CDs, commercial paper, acceptances, Treasury Bills, short-term tax-exempt notes, and Eurodollar loans.
Mortgage	A pledge of property, particularly real estate. When a loan is involved, the lender is entitled to take possession of the property if the debt is not repaid in a timely manner.
Mortgagee	The lender under a mortgage loan.
Mortgagor	The borrower under a mortgage loan.
Mutual Fund	A pooled investment in which managers buy and sell assets with the income and gains and losses accruing to the owners. May be either load (with sales fee) or no-load (no sales fee). In either case the fund stands ready to buy back its shares at their net asset value.
Net Worth Equity	A firm's or individual's residual ownership position, determined by subtracting the dollar value of liabilities from that of assets.
No-Load Fund or No-Load Mutual	A fund whose shares are bought and sold directly at the fund's NAV. Unlike a load fund, no agent or sales fee is involved.
Prepayment	The fee assessed for early liquidation of an outstanding debt.
Profit (or Loss)	Net revenues minus costs. A profit and loss statement provides a financial accounting of revenues and expenses during a specified period, i.e., three months, one year. See also Income Statement.
Proprietorship	The condition of ownership of a business entity, usually referring to sole ownership.
Rate of Return	A rate that takes into account both dividends and capital appreciation (increases in the

price of the security). A 9-percent rate of return implies that one who owns $100 worth of stock will earn a total of $9 in dividends and capital appreciation over the forthcoming year.

S Corporation — An arrangement whereby a corporation may be taxed as a partnership under the provisions of the Internal Revenue Code.

Simple Interest — Interest paid and computed only on the principal.

Stock Exchange — An organization for trading a specific list of securities over specific trading hours usually at a single location.

Tax Shelter — An investment that produces deductions from other income for the investor with a resulting savings in income taxes. Most types of tax shelters are severely restricted under the current Tax Code.

Term Insurance — A type of life insurance without a savings feature. Rates rise with age to reflect the greater probability of death. See also Whole-Life Insurance.

Universal Life — A type of life insurance in which the cash value varies with the policyholder's payments and the company's investment returns.

Variable Life — A type of life insurance in which the cash value varies with the return of the policyholder's portfolio.

Variable-Rate Mortgage — A mortgage in which the interest rate on the loan is allowed to vary with market rates.

Venture Capital — Risk capital extended to start-up or small going concerns.

Whole-Life	A type of policy that couples life insurance with a savings feature.
Insurance	Premiums are fixed, with a surplus built up in the policy's early years to meet claims that exceed premiums when the policyholders are older.
Will	A legal statement of a person's wishes with regard to the disposition of his or her property or estate at the time of death.
Yield	The return of an investment expressed as a percentage of its market value.
Yield (Current)	Current income (dividend, coupon, rent, etc.) divided by the price of the asset.

Are you ready for financial Success? To be successful in any endeavor you must have sales ability. You must be able to sell the greatest commodity in the world, yourself. You will need to be a salesperson, and good sales people are not born, they are created. The following are traits of top sales people:

1. They have an above average ability and motivation to sell.
2. They are self-starters
3. They do or act, rather than talk.
4. They enjoy selling.

They may be uncomfortable doing detailed duties, but they are excellent at selling. To be a success in life, you will need to become good at selling. All of life is about selling. And you are the product you will be selling to the world. Learn to esteem yourself daily, to be a better salesperson. To help you in this area, our book Self-Esteem, The Essence of You, and Say Goodbye to Your Smallness, Say Hello to Your Greatness is an invaluable asset.

If you believe in yourself and believe in a power greater than yourself, you will achieve financial success. Since the largest growing population in the United States today is the 85 years and older group, you will journey many times in your lifetime from success to success before you make your transition from planet earth. Often success is the result of patient persistence through failure. So do not become discouraged if you do not see instant results.

We are all a diamond in the rough, becoming our Christ-Self through our trials and tribulations. Jesus stated, "Be of good cheer, for I have conquered the world." You must never quit striving to improve yourself, or your life circumstances, even though you may have challenges, and it takes a long time to reach your goals.

You now have a blueprint to follow on How to Get and Keep Money. Reread this book often. Make notations where needed. Write to tell me of your money success stories. See yourself as a money magnet. Remember if you persist and are determined to be wealthy, I will be reading about your good deeds and accomplishments in your local newspaper. I wish for you all the Health, Wealth, Abundance, Prosperity, Joy, Peace and Love you can amass. I acknowledge you for the contribution you will make to mankind. Your success and wealth in life will be equal to the contribution you make in your service to your fellow man and woman. Great contributors to life, are rewarded with personal success, plenty of material and non material goods to share and spare. Money is an energy. It has to circulate continually. Keep your hands and your heart open to the ebb and flow of money. Dream Big, Think Big, Act Big and Be Big in your giving. Money is God in flesh. Greatness, nor money can be found in clutter, chaos, or confusion. Get clear about what you want. Be clear about your intention to have what you want. Be focused, have a high intention to serve and you will have more than enough money for yourself with plenty to spare. There is no scarcity of natural resources in the universe. I agree with Marianne Williamson and Nelson Mandela, your playing small does not serve the planet. I also believe that Greatness, Prosperity and Abundance is our natural state of being.

You are Powerful like an Eagle; you are Regal and Royal.

You were created in the image and likeness of the universe. You have wealthy lineage. Begin to act like a wealthy child. Money and wealth is your natural heritage. Claim it now. Affirm with me that you are wealthy. There are no limitations in life, except those you have imposed upon yourself. Break through your pattern of mental poverty. Be free. Say yes to Life, Say yes to God, Say yes to money and money substance. Let your spirit soar. Dream Big, Think Big. You can have it all. You deserve Money and Money substance, because You Are Worth It.

❧❧

Bibliography

Daily Word, Silent Unity, 1901 NW Blue Parkway, Unity Village, Mo 64065-0001.

Holy Bible, Kings James Version, Penguin Books USA Inc. 375 Hudson Street, New York, New York 10014

Kimbro, Dennis and Hill, Napoleon, Think and Grow Rich, A Black Choice, Ballantine Books, a division of Random House Inc. The Napoleon Hill Foundation, 1991

Posner, Mitchell J. Executive Essentials, New York: Avon Books, 1987.

Peale Norman Vincent, Plus — The Magazine of Positive Thinking, September 1995

Science of Mind, A Philosophy, A Faith, A Way of Life. September 1995, Vol. 68, No. 9, Science of Mind Publishing, P.0. Box 75127, Los Angeles, CA 90075

Sellers Reverend, Dr. Delia, Abundant Living, June 1996, P.O. Box 12525, Prescott, AZ 86304-2525

At People Skills International we coach individuals and businesses on how to break through patterns of limitation, and ceiling they have created that keep them enslaved to struggle smallness and a poverty consciousness. We provide Break Through Coaching sessions by phone on: Esteeming Yourself, Powerful Communication, Presentation Skills, Professional Empowerment, Soft Power Negotiation Skills, How to Present Oneself Favorably To Others, How to Be More Alive, on Fire, With Drive and Passion.

We have Personal Development books and tapes to assist you, they are:

Self-Esteem The Essence of You
Are You Ready for Success
Soft Power™ Negotiation Skills
How to be a Success in Business
Self-Esteem, the Essence of You
Say Goodbye to Your Smallness, Say Hello to Your Greatness
Light the Fire Within You
How to Improve Self-Esteem in the African-American Child
Anger Management Skills for Children
Anger Management Skills for Men
Anger Management Skills for Women
Stirring up the African-American Spirit

Audio cassettes
Self-Esteem, Light the Fire Within You,
Money, How to Get It, How to Keep It,

Video cassette
Self-Esteem, The Essence of You and
Say Goodbye to Your Smallness, Say Hello to Your Greatness.

Dr. Greene is available to speak to your group about Success principles and How to create wealth in your life. Call Dr. Ida Greene at (619) 262-9951 for more information; she can be reached by E-mail at idagreene@idagreene.com or on the web at www.ida-greene.com. To help you reach your goals, Intuitive Coaching is also available by phone, (619) 262-9951.

www.ingramcontent.com/pod-product-compliance
Lightning Source LLC
Chambersburg PA
CBHW031948190326
41519CB00007B/716